Ice Cream Collectibles

Ed Marks

Schiffer Publishing Ltd

4880 Lower Valley Road, Atglen, PA 19310 USA

Dedication

I dedicate this book to Phyllis, my best friend and wife for 53 years, whose support and encouragement throughout my career have been my strength and my love.

Designed by Mark David Bowyer
Type set in Lydian BT/Korinna BT

ISBN: 0-7643-1856-X
Printed in Hong Kong
1 2 3 4

Published by Schiffer Publishing Ltd.
4880 Lower Valley Road
Atglen, PA 19310
Phone: (610) 593-1777; Fax: (610) 593-2002
E-mail: Info@schifferbooks.com
Please visit our web site catalog at **www.schifferbooks.com**
We are always looking for people to write books on new and related subjects. If you have an idea for a book, please contact us at the above address.

This book may be purchased from the publisher.
Include $3.95 for shipping.
Please try your bookstore first.
You may write for a free catalog.

In Europe, Schiffer books are distributed by
Bushwood Books
6 Marksbury Avenue
Kew Gardens
Surrey TW9 4JF England
Phone: 44 (0) 20 8392 8585
Fax: 44 (0) 20 8392 9876
E-mail: Bushwd@aol.com
Free postage in the UK. Europe: air mail at cost.

Contents

Acknowledgments

Writing a book is fun, everyone told me. It's also hard work. They didn't tell me *that*. It requires loads of help; constant encouragement; and a willingness to share information, resources, family treasures, and prized possessions.

My heartfelt thanks to all my fellow Ice Screamers who did just that and more, and with special recognition to:

Mort & Bobbe Burness
August Brunner
Harold Collins
Steve Leone
John Panza
Michael & Judith Powers
Bob Sebelist
Barbara L. Sollers
Wayne Smith
Jim Spach
Richard Stalker
Joe Sutschek
Richard Uhl
Richard Warren
Robin Weir, my best friend and fellow collector from England

Introduction

ICE CREAM! Universally recognized as one of America's favorite foods. Did we create it? Not really. Then where did it come from? That's a difficult mystery to solve. Myth, rumor, and repetition in the media tell us all about Marco Polo returning from China about the end of the thirteenth century with a recipe for a sherbet-like frozen dessert. This story is often followed by the fable of Catherine De Medici taking the secret with her in the early 1550s, when she was betrothed to the future King of France. But recent research seems strongly to reveal that neither of these stories is true. So then, what really did happen?

No one really knows. It just evolved through the years and by the mid 1600s "Iced Creams" were being enjoyed by the very wealthy in Europe. Who were the "very wealthy"? The royalty, for the most part. My personal collection contains a copy of *The London Gazette*, dated September 20, 1688. The front page story states that the King entertained the previous week and among foods served to his guests was "Iced Creams."

Why was this a privilege of the royalty? Ingredients were expensive. Ice had to be imported from the Scandinavian countries and sugar was prohibitively priced as it was an imported item also. Who else could afford those luxurious commodities?

Eventually, of course, conditions improved. Prices were modified and ice cream became more available. The books on ice cream then tell of ice cream parlors developing in London and Paris in the early 1700s, and soon the fun and excitement began.

An interesting note is the fact that while we consume more vanilla ice cream today than any other flavor, back in the beginning vanilla was almost unknown. When it was eventually brought to Europe from Mexico by Cortez, it too was expensive. So the early ice cream makers, who were primarily royal confectioners, made their ice cream from the things that were readily available; they had no grocery wholesaler or frozen food dealer to buy things from.

Early ice cream flavors included things that would make you gag today—asparagus, rhubarb, brown bread, saffron, and green tea are just a few to whet your appetite. A double scoop?

Thomas Jefferson generally gets the credit for introducing vanilla to America. Word is that he brought the recipe back with him in 1784 after serving as our ambassador to France, and America loved it. We still do.

I guess if I am following the historical path, mention should be made of Philip Lenzi, a New York confectioner who generally gets credit for being the first to sell ice cream at his shop in 1777. And, if we continue on the trail, we must acknowledge the voracious appetite of George Washington, who apparently was like me in my early days. My wife used to describe me as one who, "if he didn't have ice cream by three in the afternoon started to suffer withdrawal symptoms." Maybe George and I were related. Incidentally, George Washington, not having vanilla readily available, survived on flavors such as green gage, plum, fig, and black walnut.

We can't forget Dolley Madison, who garners all the credit for being the first to serve ice cream at the White House—a fact mentioned in the media for decades but only really verified in recent years. And there was Agustus Jackson, her servant, who, when he left this duty in Washington, moved to Philadelphia and opened two ice cream parlors, the first in 1832. He became the wealthiest black person there.

Nonetheless, in those days, ice cream was still a treat and not so available as it is today. Believe it or not, ice was still a hard commodity to come by. The hand cranked ice cream freezer would not be invented until 1843. We still had a long way to go.

The evolution to the drugstore soda fountain and the inevitable ice cream treats that were offered there was on the horizon, however. The making of carbonated water had been formulated and a carbonator created in 1832. Carbonated water required the combination of sulphuric acid and ground calcium carbonate to give off the gas needed. Since this had to done at each location, where would such a chemical formulation be accomplished? Why at the local alchemist, or pharmacist, because they were the neighborhood chemists.

The first carbonated waters were considered stomach soothers, much like the antacids of today. And because America is a nation of "marketers and entrepreneurs," we soon began to flavor them to make them more appealing and to increase the demand. Then, as we were located in the drugstore, the soda fountain was born! As ice became more readily available, people began to enjoy these drinks cold.

Thus it followed, that as ice cream progressed through several stages of manufacture and distribution, we now were able to offer an ice cream parlor and soda fountain in combination. Things pretty much stayed that way until the very late 1890s, when another creative innovation appeared on the food horizon: something called the Hot Soda. The ability to sell cold drinks in the hot summer and hot drinks in the cold winter now allowed the drugstore owner to keep the fountain open all year long. You won't believe this, but the first Hot Sodas were the following: Hot Coffee, Hot Chocolate, Hot Tea, Hot Tomato Bouillon, Hot Clam Broth, and Hot Beef Broth. Scout's Honor! At their inception at the soda fountain, these drinks were considered Hot Sodas.

Logic then tells us that with all this in place, the availability of food at the counter couldn't be far behind. And it wasn't. We soon had the birth of an entirely new American creation, the Luncheonette, as well as the appearance on the scene of that wonderful star of stars: the Soda Jerk. And this leads us to another new chapter in our culture. Read on.

We had entered an era around 1905 in which this new and novel combination of drugstore soda fountain/ ice cream luncheonette/luncheonette had emerged. This phenomenon would move forward during the next fifty years and become a unique part of our American culture, spurred on to a great extent by our love and passion for ice cream—which so much of the world thought of as a special American food.

Yes, the Soda Fountain and Ice Cream Shoppe was the place to go. It was a family center, a place for the special occasion or celebration, THE place where you took your date when you wanted to impress her or show her off to your buddies. It conveyed an image of family, of warmth, of virtue, and of friendliness and was shown and portrayed as part of countless movies with love and family as their themes.

Long before fast food drive-ins arrived on the scene, families considered a drive to the ice cream store their Sunday family treat; Mom and Dad looked forward to doing this for their children all week. From this has grown a reverence for "those good old days" and for all the things associated with them. Memorabilia from this era, those things that evoke nostalgia and a fascination with days gone by, is cherished by collectors today. It was this that led me to establish the ICE SCREAMERS about 1978.

Member of the ICE SCREAMERS, a collectors' group of ice cream and soda fountain memorabilia buffs, cherish just about everything connected to that wonderful time in our history. Comprised of about 800 people from all over the United States and an enormous enthusiast from London, the group meets once a year in Lancaster, Pennsylvania for three exciting days of displays, lectures, fun, and excitement. On display are things from just about all the collectible categories illustrated in this book.

Within the pages to follow, I have focused on many "things" that I consider to be significant, but there are certainly others. As usual, different things have an appeal for different folks but I have concentrated on those items that are the most popular among collectors.

Leading the parade are ice cream dippers or scoops, pewter ice cream molds, straw holders, milkshake machines, waitress trays, and ephemera. The last category translates to "paper with an expected short life expectancy" and includes items such as postcards, trade cards, advertising, trade publications, and so forth (see more about ephemera in the next section of this book).

There are also penny licks, ice cream music such as the world famous "I Scream, You Scream, We All Scream For Ice Cream," soda fountain glassware, comic book and magazine covers with ice cream themes, and Dixie Cup lids with movie star photos.

Prices shown are approximate values and can vary based on local market demand at the time of purchase as well as on condition of the items. These prices may also differ depending on whether you are buying at an auction, from a private dealer, or on the Internet.

If all of this stimulates your interest and you would like to join or at least inquire about the ICE SCREAMERS, you can learn more about us by going to www.icescreamers.com. The fee to become a member is inexpensive; the return in satisfaction and knowledge is immeasurable. I'll keep my eye out for you.

A Word About Ephemera

A strange looking word but it pronounces easily. And what it really refers to are things that are expected to have a short life span. Meaning what? Well, things made of paper and cardboard are the first to come to mind, mostly because they have, basically, a short life span. Today's newspapers, left alone, begin to deteriorate in a matter of days. Newspapers from a hundred years ago still survive because they had high rag content. Not so, today.

And don't forget, we live in a disposable society—things aren't made to last forever. That was not the intention.

So, regarding Ice Cream collectibles, what would fall into this category of ephemera? How about:

Advertising pieces
Ice cream cartons
Picture postcards with an ice cream theme
Ice cream trade cards
Valentines with an ice cream theme
Old paper fans
Blotters
Ice cream trade catalogs and publications
Paper plates used to serve ice cream
Ladies fans with an ice cream scene
Old soda fountain menus
Photographs
Die cut advertising pieces for the fountain
Business envelopes with the company logo

This is really a very special category because these items are hard to find in good condition. Once you have found them, the secret is to preserve them in an acid free environment so they will last a long time for future collectors to enjoy.

Chapter I
Ice Cream Music

We are a music loving, ice cream loving society, And with a combination of the two, how could the composer be wrong? Over the years, many songs have been written with an ice cream theme. They have extolled love and romance, the soda fountain, parties, good times, vacations and all the pleasant things we enjoy.

Most of the music pre-dates World War II which I guess, in reality, is a reflection on how our society has changed since then. Our love of ice cream hasn't diminished but surely our taste in music has undergone many changes. Never did hear Elvis sing about ice cream or the soda fountain.

We have found, among the collectors, about 100 pieces of sheet music that fall into the category of collectibles. The challenge to increase this number remains strong.

"I Scream, You Scream, We All Scream For Ice Cream" is probably the most easily recognized and most popular piece of ice cream sheet music. Other songs that might strike a significant chord are "Oh, My Eskimo Pie" and "I'll Have Vanilla" by Eddie Cantor. One that reflects the times was "What Will We Do On A Saturday Night When The Town Goes Dry?" It was a lament on the fact that Prohibition was taking effect in 1919; the answer to the question was "eat ice cream." The results would astound you. But that's another story for another time.

"Chocolate Ripple," Piano Solo, by Thomas Filas. $15-35.

"The Ice Cream Vendor," by Charles P. Mitchell. $15-35.

"Shoot The Sherbet To Me, Herbert," by Ben Homer. $15-35.

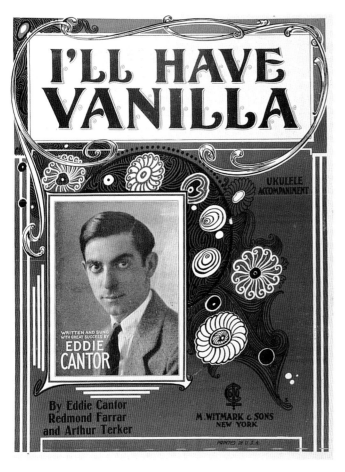

"I'll Have Vanilla," by Eddie Cantor, Redmond Farrar, and Arthur Terker. $15-35.

"O! My Eskimo Pie," by Dale Wimbrow. $15-35.

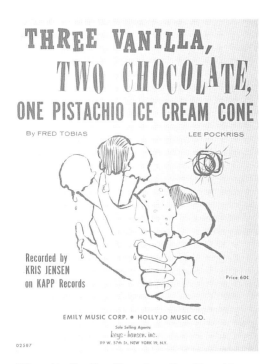

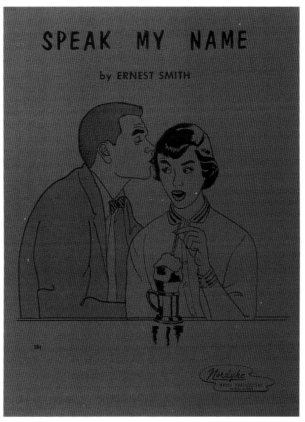

"Three Vanilla, Two Chocolate, One Pistachio Ice Cream Cone," by Fred Tobias and Lee Pockriss. $15-35.

"Speak My Name," by Ernest Smith. $15-35.

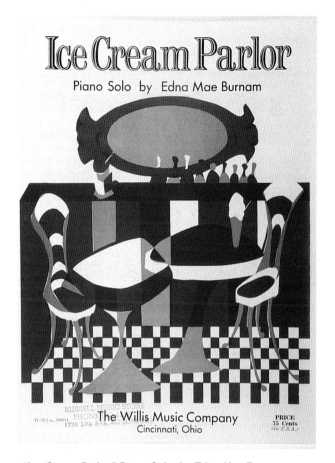

"Ice Cream Parlor," Piano Solo, by Edna Mae Burnam. $15-35.

"Ice Cream Song," by Ronnie Shannon. $15-35.

"My Hygrade Sweetie," by Baker-Evans Ice Cream Co. $15-35.

"Here Comes The Ice Cream Man," by Mae Aileen Erb. $15-35.

"Antonio," Lyrics by Robert Hargreaves and Stanley J. Damerall, Music by Tolchard Evans. $15-35.

"The Ice Cream Man," Piano Solo, with words by Irene Archer. $15-35.

"Come Have a Soda With Me," by Fred Roegge. $15-35.

"I Scream, You Scream, We All Scream For Ice Cream," by Howard Johnson, Billy Moll, and Robert King. $15-35.

"Chocolate Ice Cream Cone," by Famous Lashua. $15-35.

"Won't You Have an Ice Cream Soda With Me," by Pauline Arnold and Gladys Turner. $15-35.

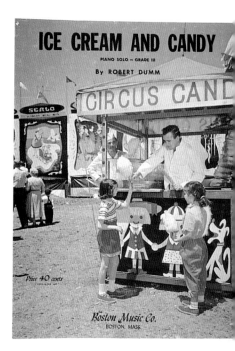

"Ice Cream and Candy," Piano Solo, by Robert Dumm. $15-35.

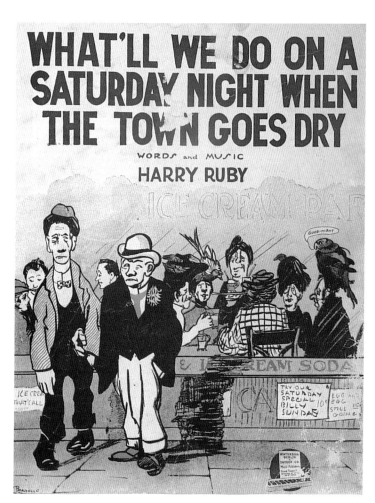

"What'll We Do On a Saturday Night When the Town Goes Dry?" by Harry Ruby. $15-35.

"OH! Mother, I'm Wild," by Howard Johnson, Harry Pease, and Eddie Nelson. $15-35.

Chapter 2
Ice Cream Comic Books

Are there any among us who haven't been bitten by the comic book bug? Surely everyone who grew up before the era of television and video games had a fondness or even a passion for comic books. Super heroes like Superman are the comic themes most generally sought. Others who are also popular reflected more of our own lifestyles. Comic characters like Henry, Tom and Jerry, Beetle Bailey, Bugs Bunny, Porky Pig, and Little Iodine are the ones that we senior citizens remember from our childhood and therefore cherish.

These characters found a special place in our hearts and our imagination at the time. While the stories themselves were not necessarily about ice cream or the soda fountain, the cover illustration was used to grab your attention. It worked.

This a very specialized collectible area. About 120 covers with this theme are known to have been created from 1930 to 1955. They are inexpensive treasures that bring us laughter, warmth, and fond memories.

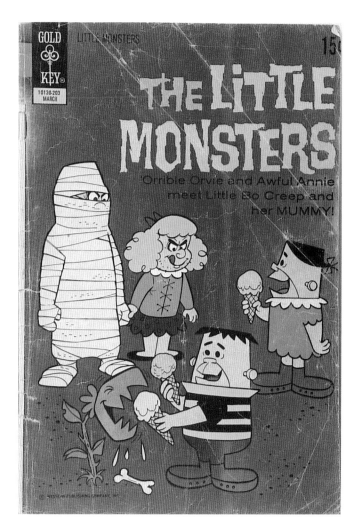

The Little Monsters. Western Publishing. $10-40.

Sparkler Comics. $10-40.

Henry. Dell Comics. $10-40.

Heathcliff's Fun House. $10-40.

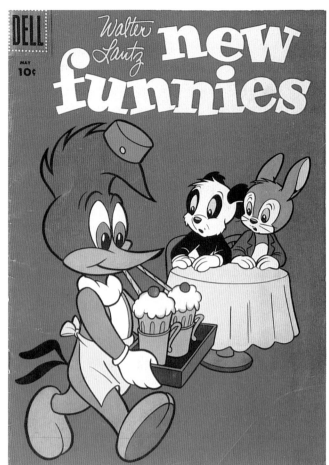

New Funnies. Dell Comics. $10-40.

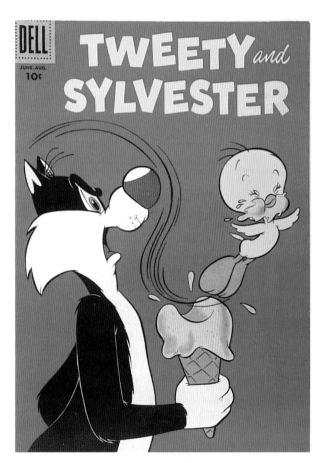

Tweety & Sylvester. Dell Comics. $10-40.

The Road Runner. $10-40.

Tom & Jerry. Dell Comics. $10-40.

Porky Pig. Dell Comics. $10-40.

Walt Disney's Comics. Dell Comics. $10-40.

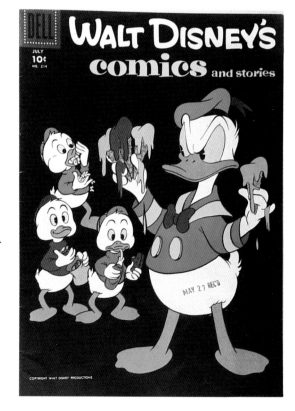

Richie Rich. Harvey Comics. $10-40.

Audrey & Melvin. Harvey Comics. $10-40.

Archie. The Archie Series. $10-40.

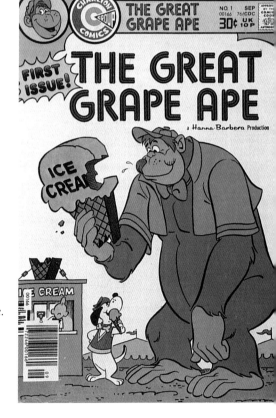

The Great Grape Ape.
Charlton Comics.
$10-40.

Andy Panda. Walter
Lentz. $10-40.

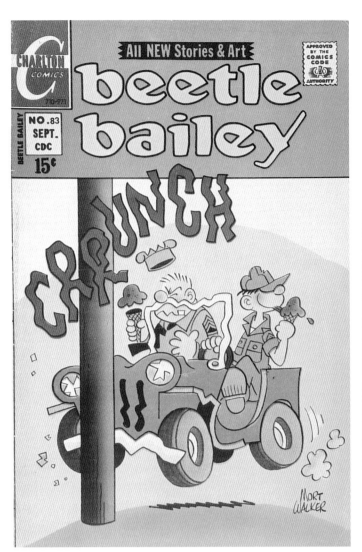

Beetle Bailey. Charlton Comics. $10-40.

Bugs Bunny. Dell Comics. $10-40.

Little Iodine, by Jimmy Hatlo. Dell Comics. $10-40.

Chapter 3
Penny Licks

Of all the collectibles chosen as topics for this book, the one that has truly captured the imagination of collectors and caused much excitement is the penny lick.

Making ice cream in the early 1800s was a chore unto itself. The hand cranked ice cream freezer had not yet been invented and ice cream making was a slow process. How to dispense and sell it was another matter. The creation of the ice cream cone in 1896 in America was still many years away. Street vendors, who were very popular in London, Paris, Rome and Naples, needed something to put their ice cream in so that they could serve it to their customers. Quite often, small cups made of crystal or porcelain and having one or two handles were used in Naples.

The price of manufacturing glass in England became less expensive after the Glass Excise Tax was abolished in 1845. Production of glass became more efficient. The penny lick, a small stemmed glass generally made of a poor quality glass, then became quite popular with the vendors, who felt they could afford to use these to dispense ice cream. Three sizes became standard for use: the small halfpenny lick, the penny lick, and the twopenny lick, which was the largest. As the use of penny licks increased, manufacturing designs changed and eventually they began looking very similar to shot glasses used at bars—they had thick bottoms that created the optical illusion of a large portion. In reality, the portions were quite small. The illusion of ice cream standing tall was helped to a degree by the twisting of the peak, very similar to that used by soft serve ice cream stands today.

Why the name penny lick? It actually referred to how the ice cream was consumed. The container was not edible, like an ice cream cone, and there was no spoon given to help with eating. So you "licked" it clean, " penny a lick," and gave it back to the vendor to use again. Obviously, this meant that you could not walk down the avenue eating your ice cream—you had to stay by the vending cart and finish your treat. Penny licks were featured in many of the newspapers of the day, and one of the more

Above and below:
Half pence, penny lick, two pence. $75-150 each.

famous is an 1868 illustration in *Harper's Weekly* showing penny licks being used in New York City. The earliest known drawing of their use was by Barolomeo Pinellie of Naples, in 1817.

Penny licks remained popular for a long time, even though they were the cause of many health problems, all stemming from the fact that most vendors seldom washed them as they were passed from one customer to the next. In London, penny licks were finally prohibited in 1926 because it was felt that they caused the spread of many diseases, particularly tuberculosis. In the United States, street vendors were much quicker to convert to ice cream cones because many of their customers simply walked off with the penny licks. In addition, children had a tendency to drop the penny licks and they would shatter.

These items were first brought to our attention as a collectible about 1985. Penny licks were selling in London then for about $1.50 each. In today's market, $75.00 to $145.00 is not unusual. Many unscrupulous dealers are offering up eggcups, drinking glasses, and candleholders as penny licks, particularly on the Internet. Newly made reproductions made in France and Portugal have also appeared, so be cautious.

An assortment of sizes. $75-175 each.

Half pence and penny lick. $85-150 each.

Two pence and penny lick. $85-145.

Chapter 4
Magazine Covers

Magazine covers with an ice cream or soda fountain theme as the eye catcher are a popular collectible. They date back to the early 1900s and the theme is still being used today by many publications worldwide.

Until the 1960s, the majority of magazines published were "family magazines." They were focused on family values and topics of interest to the housewife and mother, and many were delivered directly to the home by "magazine carriers," just as we had paper carriers in years gone by. The housewives and mothers were the primary buyers of these magazines. If not delivered, they could be bought at the corner store. And so, bearing an ice cream theme, magazines appealed to the fun, the pleasures, and the wholesomeness that family values incorporated.

While many of these magazines are no longer being published, their names will evoke the images from earlier days. Some that you may recall are *The Saturday Evening Post*, *Farmers Wife*, *Colliers*, *Modern Priscilla*, *Ladies Home Journal*, *Life*, *Farm & Home*, *Liberty*, *Woman's World*, *McCalls*, *Country Gentleman*, *People's Home Journal*, and *Good Housekeeping*.

Colliers and the *Saturday Evening Post* were the two most prominent magazines to feature ice cream and soda fountain themes. The Saturday Evening Post also had the distinction of having used some Norman Rockwell pictures as cover themes. Several of the magazine covers highlighted movie stars. In those days, sports stars went unnoticed.

Collier's. June 9, 1951. $15-35.

Collier's. May 30, 1953. $15-35.

Collier's. July 17, 1920. $15-35.

Collier's. June 17, 1922. $15-35.

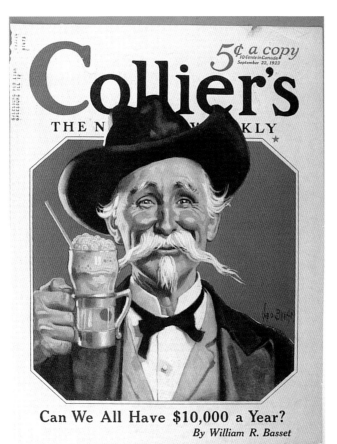

Collier's. September 22, 1923. $15-35.

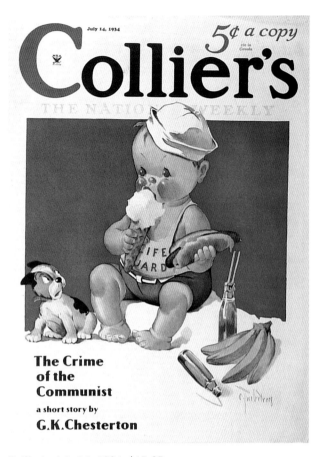

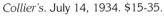
Collier's. July 14, 1934. $15-35.

Collier's. October 16, 1937. $15-35.

Collier's. October 1, 1938. $15-35.

Collier's. May 3, 1941. $15-35.

Collier's. August 30, 1941. $15-35.

Collier's. September, 22, 1945. $15-35.

Collier's. September 4, 1948. $15-35.

Life. June 17, 1920. $15-35.

Life. September 18, 1924. $15-35.

Life. August, year unknown. $15-35.

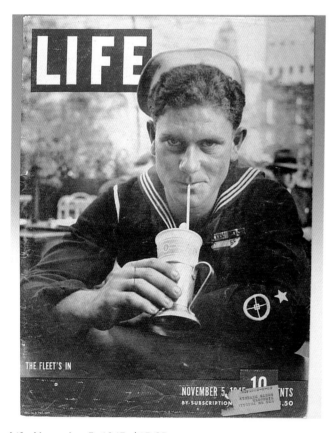

Life. November 5, 1945. $15-35.

Life. January 18, 1943. $15-35.

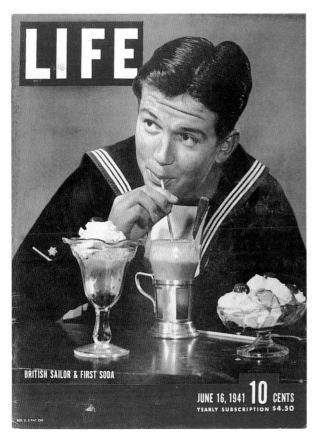

Life. June 16, 1941. $15-35.

Life. May 19, 1947. $15-35.

Sunday Magazine of the Sunday Record-Herald.
July 18, 1909. $15-35.

Saturday Evening Post. October 12, 1946. $15-35.

Saturday Evening Post. October 11, 1947. $15-35.

Saturday Evening Post. March 17, 1917. $15-35.

Saturday Evening Post. July 29, 1905. $15-35.

Saturday Evening Post. July 27, 1912. $15-35.

Saturday Evening Post. August 12, 1922. $15-35.

Saturday Evening Post. September, 21, 1935. $15-35.

Saturday Evening Post. September 16, 1922. $15-35.

Saturday Evening Post. July 29, 1944. $15-35.

Saturday Evening Post. September 22, 1951. $15-35.

Saturday Evening Post. June 27, 1953. $15-35.

Saturday Evening Post. August 16, 1952. $15-35.

Woman's World. July 1939. $15-35.

Ladies' Home Journal. August 1926. $15-35.

Ladies' Home Journal. July 1923. $15-35.

Ladies' Home Journal.
November 1931. $15-35.

Ladies' Home Journal. August 1937. $15-35.

Ladies' Home Journal. September 1952. $15-35.

People's Home Journal. May 1929. $15-35.

Good Housekeeping. July 1907. $15-35.

Good Housekeeping. Unknown date. $15-35.

McCall's Magazine. July 1913. $15-35.

McCall's. Unknown date. $15-35.

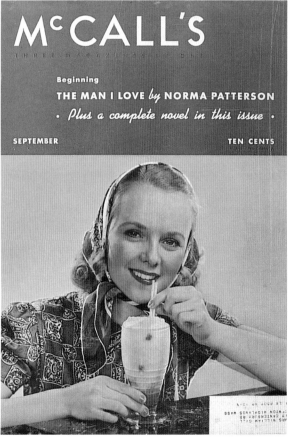

McCall's. September 1939. $15-35.

Time. September 7, 1953. $15-35.

Country Gentleman. June 1936. $15-35.

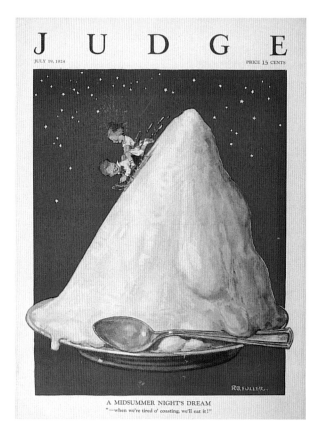

Judge. July 19, 1924. $15-35.

Wall Street's Prophets Without Profits
Earl Blackwell: The Godfather of the Social Climbers
My Ten Best Movies, by Woody Allen

40 CENTS

AUGUST 3, 1970

NEW YORK

Everything
You Always
Wanted To
Know About
Ice Cream
But Were
Too Fat
To Ask

Explained
By Gael
Greene

New York. August 3, 1970. $15-35.

WEEK ENDING JUNE 25, 1927

5¢ **Liberty**

A Weekly for Everybody

TRY OUR SPECIAL CUPID'S MARSHMALLOW SUNDAE

"His Bachelor Supper"

Beginning **THE DEVIL'S MANTLE** *by* **FRANK L. PACKARD**
A Serial of Mystery and Adventure in the South Seas
also **THE RED KNIGHT** *of* **GERMANY,** *the* **STORY** *of* **RICHTHOFEN**

Liberty. June 25, 1927. $15-35.

Farm and Home. June 1924. $15-35.

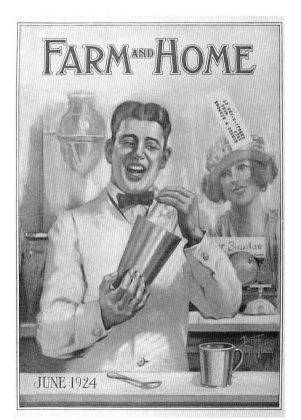

FARM AND HOME

JUNE 1924

Chapter 5
Ice Cream Scoops

Called ice cream dippers or ice cream scoops, these surely comprise the most popular category of ice cream collectibles. With several hundred different models to attract attention there is no shortage of interest.

William Clewell, of Reading, Pennsylvania, is considered the creator of the first ice cream disher. Prior to this, ice cream was neither dipped nor scooped, but rather "spooned" from the pot into the serving dish. Clewell had a confectionery store in Reading and was annoyed with the inefficiency of the system, so he worked to find a better way. In doing so, he came up with the disher, for which he received a patent on May 3, 1878. He had them manufactured by Valentine Clad, a tinsmith from Philadelphia.

Basically, Clewell's disher consisted of a conical mold with a key operated scraper that released the ice cream onto a plate. It was well received by other confectioners and within a very short time several other manufacturers had similar devices on the market.

Clewell's disher was, as mentioned, conical in shape with a key release. It was essentially made of tin, which made it subject to rust and deterioration. Though well over one hundred years old, these items are not too difficult to find at antique stalls and flea markets today, as they are not considered too desirable. Therefore, they are not too expensive. These early ones still are in the $40.00 to $75.00 range. Collectors prefer things that are bright and shiny. Therefore, dippers that are bronzed or chromed command more attention and higher prices.

Ice cream dippers/scoops differ from each other in three regards. The first is the shape of the portion, which can be round, conical, or a flat slab. The second distinction is found in the size of the portion. Generally, on the scraper blade inside the dipper you will find a number that indicates the number of portions that particular scoop will yield from a one quart container. The numbers run as follows: 6-8-10-12-16-20-40. The smaller the number, the larger the portion; the larger the number, the smaller the portion. In general, the largest and the smallest are those that are in greatest demand with collectors.

The third distinction among dippers/scoops lies with what is called the release mechanism. This refers to the method used to get the ice cream out and onto the plate or ice cream cone. The early ones had a turnkey. Some have a squeeze handle, while the majority have a thumb lever, which causes the action.

Several hundred patents were issued for ice cream dippers. For some reason, change and improvement in these seemed to appeal to those with a creative flair. In a way, this was a testament to the increasing popularity of ice cream, the ice cream luncheonette, and soda fountain as part of our American culture.

Some of the names of dipper makers you will find most frequently are:

Round: Arnold, Benedict, Erie Specialty, Geer Manufacturing, Gem Spoon, Hamilton Beach, Quick and Easy, and Gilchrist

Conical: Benedict, V.Clad, Erie Specialty, Geer, Kingery, Quick and Easy

Square or Rectangular: Automatic Cone Co., Cake Cone Co., Jiffy Dispenser, Mayer Manufacturing Co.

Novelty: Bohlig Manufacturing Co., Dover Manufacturing Co., Fisher Motor Co., J.D. Geer Co., Gilchrist, Hamilton Beach, Manos Novelty Co., and Mosteller

Non-Mechanical: Benedict, Gilchrist, Rainbow and Zeroll.

There are others out there as well, but this will give you an idea of what you might find. In addition, there are also many dippers/scoops that are very valuable collectibles and for whom the maker is "unknown." Now that's a discovery!

For some strange, unaccountable reason, an unusual number of new patents was issued to people who lived in the western part of Pennsylvania. Perhaps creating ice cream dippers/scoops was a better alternative to working in the steel mills.

Creativity in dippers just about disappeared after Sherman Kelly introduced the Zeroll in 1935. Its efficiency was beyond question and the fact that it is still in such demand within the ice cream dipping trade no doubt accounts for the lack of new dippers appearing on the scene.

In the past twenty years—since the inception of the Ice Screamers—interest in dippers has grown. In 1986, Ice Screamer Wayne Smith published his book on *Ice Cream Dippers*, which has become the collectors' bible. With attention focused on these by both the club and the book, interest has intensified and prices have soared almost ridiculously. A Manos heart shaped dipper which at one time was less the $100.00 peaked out close to $17,000.00 at the high point. Oh well, it's only money.

V. Clad Co., Philadelphia Pennsylvania, 1876 patent date; inventor William Clewell. 8-1/2", tubular steel. Handle, conical bowl. $45-60.

Unknown maker. 8", steel loop handle; turnkey release. Handle marked "Royal." c. 1900-1910. $45-60.

Unknown maker. Pint-hand packed; key release. c. 1900-1910. $55-60.

Unknown maker. 8", loop handle, conical bowl; key release. c. 1910. $65-70.

Unknown maker. 8", squeeze handle. c. 1890-1900. $145-190.

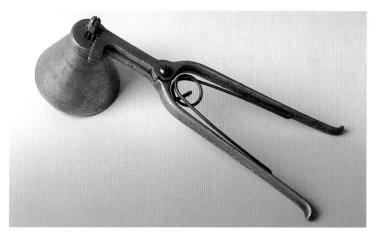

Unknown maker. Patented 1901; inventor Maximilian Bach. 10",
steel handle marked E & Co; conical bowl. $125-145.

Unknown maker. 8", squeeze handle; conical bowl. c. 1910-1915.
$145-160.

Gilchrist No. 30; patented 1914. 10-1/2", squeeze handle, conical
bowl, brass and nickel plated. $55-65.

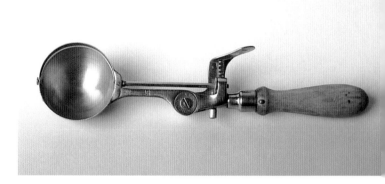

Erie Specialty Co., Erie, Pennsylvania, patented 1915; inventor
Edwin Walker. 10-1/2", thumb plate release. Bottom shank marked
"Quick & Easy." $125-145.

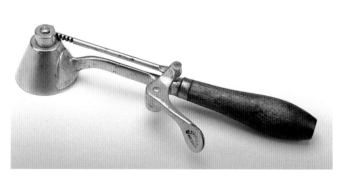

Gilchrist No 33, Pyramid Shape Ice Cream Disher, patented
September 1914; inventor Raymond Gilchrist. 10-1/2",
conical bowl, brass and nickel plated, wood handle.
$110-140.

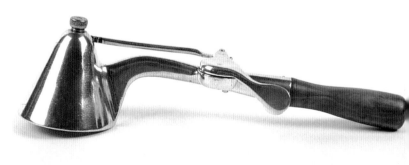

Erie Specialty No. 187, Erie, Pennsylvania, patented May 1915; inventor
Edwin Walker. 10-1/2" cone shape. $135-160.

Erie Specialty Co., Erie, Pennsylvania, patented May 1915. 10-1/2",
brass and nickel plated, Quick & Easy Series. $145-160.

"New Method" Ice Cream Disher, Dover Mfg. Co., Dover; inventors
George Holmes and Frank Grant. Known as the Dover Slicer.
11-1/2". c. 1924. $225-300.

Indestructo No. 4, Benedict Mfg. Co., Syracuse, New York, patented July 1928. $110-125.

Top: Mosteller Mfg. Co., Syracuse, New York. Conical bowl, brass and nickel plated. c. 1900-1910. $125-150. Bottom: Delmonico Disher, Marked N & Co Delmonico. Brass and nickel plated, conical bowl. c. 1900-1910. $125-150.

Manos Novelty Co., Toronto, Canada, patented 1925 by John Manos. 11", brass and nickel plated, heart shaped bowl. The rarest and most desirable scoop. $8,000-12,000.

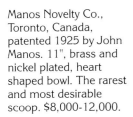

Gilchrist No 31 "Banana Split," Gilchrist Co., Newark, New Jersey, patented 1915. 11-1/2", oval bowl. $700-800.

"NO-PAK 31," Hamilton Beach Co. Racine, Wisconsin, patented 1932; inventor John Cox. 11", bowl, round with hole cut in side. $450-500.

Unknown maker, patented 1932; inventor Ernest Millo. 10", bowls disc shaped, used to fit Dixie Cup type container. $400-500.

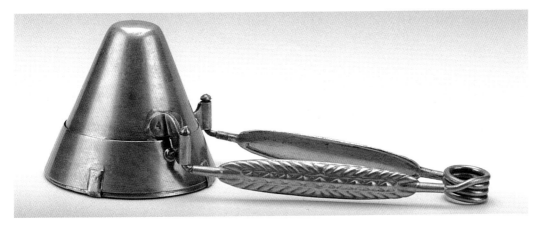

Kingery's Rapid Ice Cream Disher, Kingery Mfg. Co., Cincinnati, Ohio, patented 1894; inventor Edson Baughman. 8-1/2", handle squeeze type, nickel plated metal, bowl rotates when handle is squeezed. $175-250.

Ice Cream Scoops 37

Delmonico Disher. 8", solid brass and nickel plated, conical bowl. c. 1900-1910 $125-150.

"Clipper," F.S. Co., Troy, New York, patented 1915; inventor Rasmus Nielson. 11", Bowl round, handle wood, brass and nickel plated. $95.

Rainbow Spade. Bowl with curved sides used to make multi-flavored "Rainbow" cones. c. 1935. $75.

Benedict Mfg. Co., East Syracuse, New York. 9-1/2", used to pack ice cream into cartons, Bakelite handle. c. 1935-1940. $40.

Unknown maker, patented 1910; inventor Albert Daniel. 9", brass and nickel plated, handle wood, inverted cone bowl. $850-950.

Unknown maker. 10", brass and nickel plated; bowl round and has point on outside for making "Sundae Creams." $450-500.

Unknown maker and inventor, no known patent date. 10". $800-950.

Unknown maker and inventor, no known patent date. 9". $900-1,200.

Mosteller Mfg. Co., Chicago, Illinois, patented 1906; inventor Dosier Mosteller. 11", round bowl, aluminum and nickel plated brass; bowl flips upside down when thumb lever is depressed. $375-425.

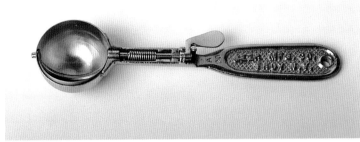

Geer Mfg. Co., Troy New York, patented 1905; inventor Rasmus Nielson. 9-1/2", bowl has a double scraper $300-350.

Myers Mfg. Co., Galesburg, Illinois, patented 1936; inventor Louis Myers. 8-1/2", bowl round, thumb piece marked Myers Deluxe Disher. $75.

Unknown maker and inventor, patent date c. 1925. $600-640.

Erie Specialty Co., Erie, Pennsylvania, No 486. $150-200.

Erie Specialty Co., Erie, Pennsylvania, patented 1915; inventor Edwin Walker. "Quick & Easy" series, bowl round. $175-225.

Unknown maker and patent date. 8", used to fill cones.
c.1938-1940. $950-1,250.

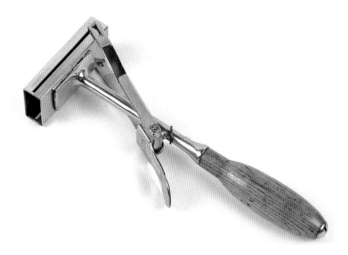

Unknown maker. Bowl rectangular, brass and nickel plated.
Used to make ice cream sandwiches. c. 1920-1930. $1,200 -1,500.

Unknown maker. Used to make ice
cream sandwiches.
c. 1924-1930. $775-800.

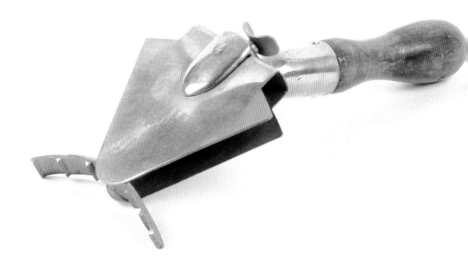

Pi-Alamoder Inc., St. Louis, Missouri, patented 1926; inventors Harlan Gardner & Alvin
Olafson. 8-1/2", aluminum, used for Pie-ala-Mode and special triangular containers.
$2,200-2,600.

Unknown maker. 8", used to make ice cream sandwiches.
c. 1920-1930. $525-700.

Unknown maker. 11", Pint
Packer. c. 1920-1930.
$350-500.

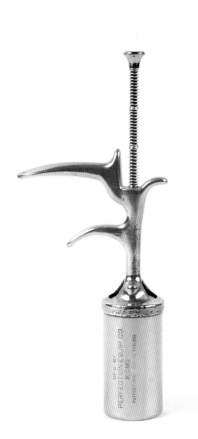

Perfection Equipment Co., Kansas City, Missouri, patented 1933; inventor Ora E. Harris. 3-1/2", cylinder bowl, plunger mechanism for making "Sky-Hi Cones." $550-700.

Unknown maker. Plunger mechanism, cylindrical. c. 1920-1930. $475-575.

General Ice Cream Corp., Schenectady, New York, patented 1925; inventor William Daly. Cylinder bowl. $425-525.

Unknown maker. Dispenses ice cream cylinder shape cones similar to old MellOroll cones. c. 1930-1940. $250-350.

Ice cream sandwich makers, from left:

Philadelphia Ice Cream Cone Machinery Co., Philadelphia, Pennsylvania. "Polar Pak" disher. c. 1932. $450-575.

"Rainbow Ice Cream Dispenser," Cake Cone Co., St. Louis, Missouri. c. 1920-1930. $375-400.

Automatic Cone Co., Cambridge, Massachusetts; inventor James Denaro. Front marked Icypi, Automatic Cone Co. c. 1924-1930. $300-400.

Jiffy Dispenser Co., Aurora, Illinois. Square, curved, front marked Jiffy Dispenser Co., curved to fit side of container used to make ice cream sandwiches. c. 1925. $250-275.

Unknown maker. Thought to be an "Original Ranch System" scoop. $1,000-1,200.

Jack Frost, handle Bakelite and marked "Jack Frost Pat. Applied For." $1,200-1,300.

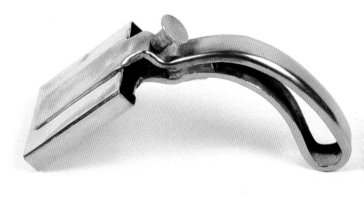

Unknown maker. Ice cream sandwich maker; pistol handle, flat scoop. $250-300.

Unknown maker. Slicer, 10", wooden handle. c. 1930. $450-550.

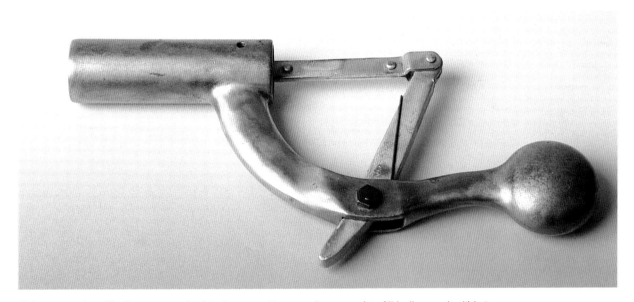

Unknown maker. 9", aluminum, cylindrical, no markings; perhaps used to fill hollow and edible ice cream containers. c. 1922-1930. $1,000-1,200.

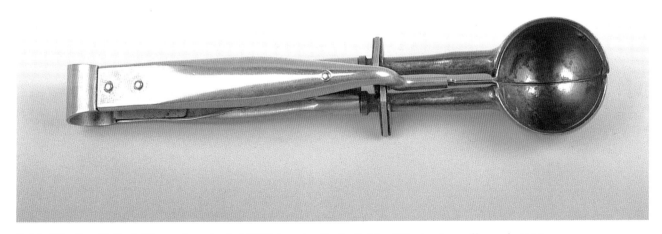

Bohlig Mfg. Co., St. Paul, Minnesota, patented 1908; inventor Martin Bohlig. 10", aluminum. Unusual scoop, bowl divides in half when handle is squeezed allowing the ice cream to drop through bottom. $1,200-1,300.

Chapter 6
Ice Cream Cup Lids

The lids or caps on ice cream cups were at times both colorful and informative. Within the limited round space available, most, if not all the following data was squeezed into the small surface area: a) the name and location of the dairy or ice cream company, b) an original design for their logo, c) net weight of the contents, d) a promotional slogan, and e) the flavor of the ice cream. In a few instances, even the price of 5 cents would be shown.

However, if the cup had been manufactured and franchised through the Dixie Cup Co., then you also received an attractive color picture on the underside of the lid. To insure that the ice cream was not in direct contact with the lithographic ink, an easily removed semi-transparent thin paper cover was made to adhere to the waxed color picture. This novel sanitary shield was patented by the Individual Drinking Cup Co., as the Dixie Cup Co. was then called.

As a result, Dixie Cups containing ice cream were by far the largest seller in the retail ice cream cup market from 1930 to 1954. During this time, some non-Dixie products also appeared featuring the popular Skippy character of the 1930s as well as some Walt Disney characters. The Kalix Cup Co. pictured the Little Rascals, but all of these images were on the top side of the lid.

An attempt to circumvent the Dixie patent was made in the 1940s by the Lilly Cup Co., when they issued an interesting series of twenty-six famous American Shrines. The company used two attached lids that were folded in such a way that the clean blank underside of the second lid was in direct contact with the ice cream. This effort, as worthy as it was, did not win favor with the youngsters.

There is no doubt that the following proud proclamation made by the Dixie Cup Co. in their early 1940s ads was justified:

> "In the whole broad field and long history of advertising promotions, there is no product, other than the franchise Dixie Cup for ice cream, which has become known to the buying public by the name of the container rather than by the nature of the contents."

After considerable research and a trial run, the Dixie picture lids started out in 1930 with a well-advertised, two year program utilizing twenty-four circus animals and performers of the Dixie Circus radio programs, which was airing at the time. The U.S. President lids was a supplemental 1931 issue, made exclusively for Aristocrat Ice Cream. In 1932, a nature series of birds, dogs, fish, and butterflies was used by Dixie as an educational feature.

In 1933, the first of twenty-four Hollywood movie stars were depicted and their success resulted in movie stars and cowboys becoming a regular annual feature up to the end. The last issue, in 1954, numbered only eighteen lids and they were in a 3D action format. Other supplemental issues of twenty-four lids were occasionally added to the twenty-four movie stars. These included mystery faces in 1934, World War II related lids from 1941 to 1944, and baseball players in 1952 to 1954.

During this twenty-five year picture lid era, the Dixie Cup Co. provided a lid-premium redemption program. Slotted album holders were made available at the retail site for the consumer. Returning this album with the proper

Dixie advertising posters. $30 each.

amount of lids inserted in the slots would get you a large and beautiful color photo of your choice. In 1954, the only premium offered (using the mail) was a stereo viewer for the left and right tab lids needed to achieve the 3D effect.

After 1954, the Dixie Lid premium redemption program continued via the U.S. Mail. Various toys, games, and many other prizes pictured on the top side of the blank bottom lids were offered simply for the postage costs and return of the lid. To a lesser extent, the Lilly Cup Co. was also involved in this type of mail order redemption.

These novelty lids appear to have ended by 1965.

1930, Horse, $6; 1931, Ringmaster; President Wilson, $10-12; 1932, Bass Fish, $5.

1925 *Saturday Evening Post* ad for Dixie Cups. $8.

1933, Actress Myrna Loy, $8; 1934, Jean Harlow, Jackie Cooper, Mystery Movie Star, $8 each; 1935, Katherine Hepburn, $8.

1936, Buster Crabbe, $10; 1937, William Boyd, Hop-A-Long Cassidy, $5-12; 1938, Gene Autry, $5-12; 1939, Roy Rogers $5-12.

1943, Alice Faye, Guadalcanal, $5 each; 1944, Betty Grable, Military Bomber, $10-20 each; 1945, Carmen Miranda, $15.

1940, Maureen O'Hara, $8; 1941, Lucille Ball, U.S.S. Saratoga, $5-7 each; 1942, Sonja Henie, Paratrooper, $5 each.

1946, Veronica Lake and Alan Ladd, $8 each; 1947, Gabby Hayes, $15; 1949, Judy Garland, $12; 1949, Bing Crosby, $15; 1950, Elizabeth Taylor, $10.

1951, Dean Martin and Jerry Lewis, $18 each; 1951, Clark Gable, Monte Irwin, $12 each; 1953, John Wayne, Warren Spahn, $17-35 each; 1954, 3-D Cyd Charisse, Gil McDougald, $8-20 each.

1946 "Extra Large" John Wayne, $9; 1959, Sealtest Strawberry, Camera ad, $10 each; 1960, Pike's Peak, $8.

1945, uncut Hoodsie Sheet, $15.

Lilly Cup lids,
$3 each.

Roy Rogers "Trade- In"
lids, $5 each.

Non Lilly Cup lids: Skippy Ice Cream, Nelson Ice Cream, $5 each.

Chapter 7
Ice Cream Vending Vehicles

Back about 1840 and starting in New York City, vendors began selling ice cream on street corners from their carts and wagons. Ice cream vending became a very popular business. The first of these vendors were black. As more immigrants came to America, it became an entry level occupation passing to the Irish, the Italians, and finally to the Greeks, who became quite attracted to the ice cream and confectionery side of things and who, even today, are steadfastly rooted to it.

As the population increased, as cities grew, as neighborhoods developed, and as transportation improved, we also saw emerge in the early 1930s the vending truck and the neighborhood Good Humor Man. He, and people like him, became someone that families looked forward to seeing each day during the summer months.

Vending carts and Good Humor type vehicles are a specialized collectible for people to enjoy today.

Italian street vender, unknown maker, wooden. 24" x 17" x 8". $150-200.

Early ice cream vending wagon replication, unknown maker. 18" x 8" x 7". $90-110.

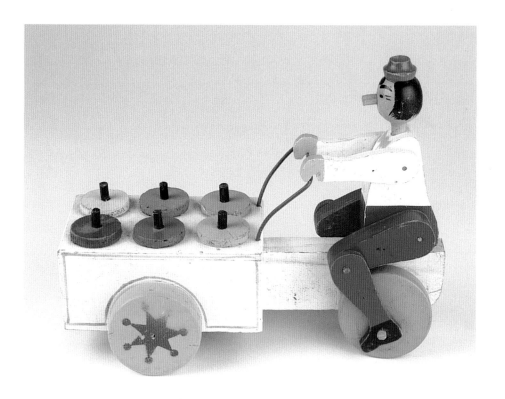

Wooden push toy, unknown maker, c. 1915. 14" x 5". $35-50.

Ice cream push toy made in China, c. 1950. 4" x 4" x 2". $15. Ice cream
push toy made in Japan, c. 1950. 3-1/2" x 4" x 2". $20.

Courtland Ice Cream windup truck, c. 1935. 8-1/2" x 2" x 3". $65-85. Arctic Ice Cream
windup truck, c. 1938, maker unknown. 6" x 3" x 4". $45-60.

Self propelled toy vehicle, maker unknown,
c. 1970. 7" x 6" x 5". $20-30.

Toy ice cream trucks, maker unknown,
c. 1950. $65-85 each.

Good Humor truck with driver, maker unknown, c. 1960. $55.
Howard Johnson, 28 Flavors truck, maker unknown,
c. 1960. $55-75.

Good Flavor Ice Cream self propelled truck, made in Japan, maker
unknown, c. 1960. $55-75.

Ice Cream 5¢ windup cycle, Courtland Toy, c. 1950. $100-125.

Fresh, Delicious Ice Cream truck, made in Japan, c. 1960.
9" x 3-1/2" x 3". $30-45.

Delicious Ice Cream vending truck, made in
Japan, c. 1970. 12" x 3-1/2" x 5". $55-65.

H.P. Hood toy truck bank, Limited Edition by Kenworth,
c. 1957. 7" x 4"x 2-1/2". $35-45.

Ice Cream All Flavors toy, maker unknown, c. 1960. $15. Bugs Bunny Ice Cream truck, plastic, Hong Kong, c. 1970. 6" x 2" x 2-1/2". $25-35.

Aesthetic Specialties Ice Cream & Sarsaparilla delivery truck, Limited Edition, c. 1980. 12" x 7" x 6". $85-100.

Good Humor trucks, assorted sizes, commemorative, c. 1985-1995. $75-125 each.

Chapter 8
Ice Cream Figurines

This is a fun category, It generally does not require a major investment and you can find these nice things in a variety of stores all year long. It is not necessary to go antiquing or flea marketing. My wife and I stopped collecting these when we reached about 400. The reason was that we had them on display all over the house and finally ran out of windowsills and mantle places to put them! Collectibles like this need to displayed, not packed away. As with everything else, there are some exceptions to the price guide. Lladro's from Spain are beautiful but can be expensive.

Windup toy monkey with ice cream cone, 7-1/2" tall, Japanese, c. 1955. $115-135.

Limoges ice cream cone, 2" wide, c. 1995. $40-45. Limoges ice cream on a stick, 2" wide, c. 1995. $40-45. Lladro black girl with dog, 7" tall, c. 1990. $125-145.

Lladro Monday's Child, 6" tall, c. 1992. $135-150.

Lladro Ice Cream Vendor, 7-1/2" x 5", c. 1985. $240-275.

Facchino papier mâché boy holding ice cream cone, English, c. 1930. 22" x 16" x 5". $1,500-2,000.

Facchino papier mâché girl holding ice cream cone, English, c. 1930. 22" x 16" x 5". $1,500-2,000

Askeys papier mâché young man holding ice cream cone, English, c. 1930. 16" x 24" x 9". $2,000-3,000.

Assortment of hand cranked ice cream freezer figurines, c. 1990-1995. 2" to 4" tall. $20-30 each.

Black children enjoying ice cream, c. 1990s.
3"- 4" tall. $20-25 each.

Handcrafted pewter ice cream vendor scene,
c. 1990. 7" tall. $110-140.

Italian street vendor musical toy, battery operated, made in
Japan, c. 1985. 9" x 12" x 4". $55-70.

Clowns with ice cream, c. 1990. 4" -11" tall. $15-45 each.

Norman Rockwell ice cream soda fountain scenes, c. 1957-1958. 4" x 5". $55-70 each.

Norman Rockwell ice cream scene, c. 1952. 4" x 5". $65-80.

Assorted soda fountain scenes, c. 1975-1990. 3-1/2" x 3-1/2". $65-75 each.

Norman Rockwell ice cream soda fountain scene, c. 1953. 6" x 5". $75-90.

Alex Hayley "Remembers" Collection, A Day in the Park, c. 1988. 3" x 5". $40-50.

"Sundae Afternoon," English street vending scene, c. 1990. $55-70.

Royal Dalton ice cream vending wagons, c. 1985-1995. 2" x 3-1/2". $45-50 each.

Chapter 9
Children's Books

Ice cream is a special treat for just about everyone. With children, it is a *very* special treat. Countless authors have capitalized on the fact that as children learn to read and begin their school years, stories about ice cream or stories with an ice cream theme will appeal to them and help focus their attention. These stories play on children's imagination and their desire for fun, laughter, and good times. With ice cream, how can they go wrong?

Underdog And The Disappearing Ice Cream, a Golden Book. $15-25.

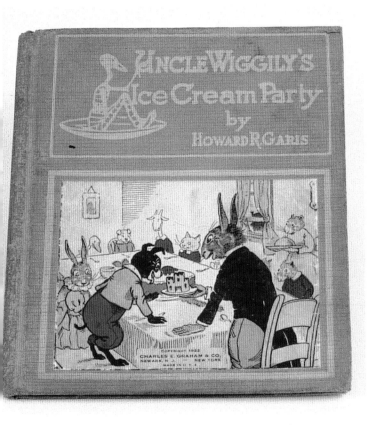

Uncle Wiggily's Ice Cream Party, by Howard Garis. $15-25.

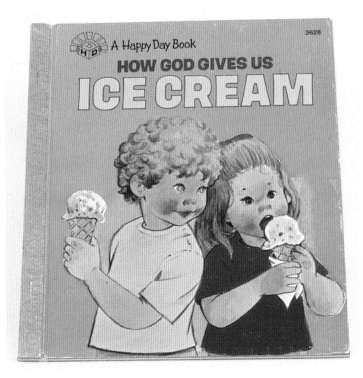

How God Gives Us Ice Cream, A Happy Day Book. $15-25.

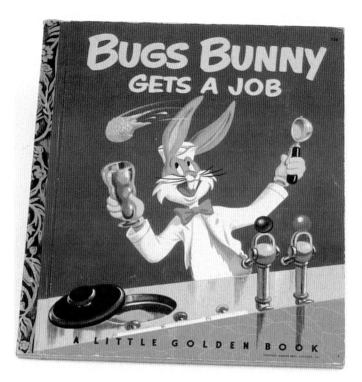

Bugs Bunny Gets a Job, A Golden Book. $15-25.

Henry Goes To A Party, Wonder Books. $15-25.

Ice Cream Soup, based on a story by Jack Kent. $15-25.

Rugrats Ice Cream Fun Day, by Nickelodeon. $15-25.

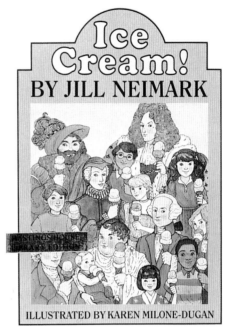

Ice Cream Soup, by Frank Modell. $15-25.

Ice Cream, by Jill Neimark. $15-25.

Ice Cream For Breakfast, by Leslie Levine. *Yum, Yum, Yum*, by Andy Warhol. $15-25.

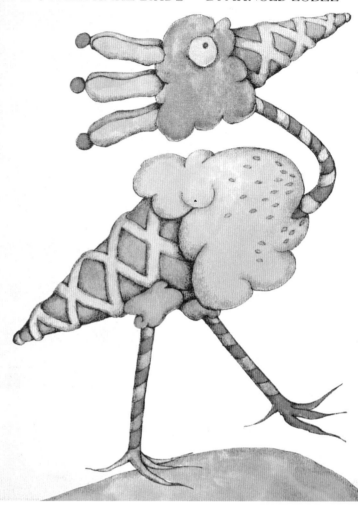

THE ICE-CREAM CONE COOT
AND OTHER RARE BIRDS   BY ARNOLD LOBEL

Tabitha Tabby's Fantastic Flavor, A Golden Tell-A-Tale Book. $15-25.

The Ice-Cream Cone Coot And Other Rare Birds, by Arnold Lobel. $15-25.

Ghouls Don't Scoop Ice Cream, by Dudley & Jones. *The Good Humor Man*, A Little Golden Book. $15-25.

Chapter 10
Pewter Ice Cream Molds

Up until 1965, one of the most delightful ice cream treats you could buy was called Fancy Forms. Fancy Forms were molded ice creams and were offered not only by all the major ice cream manufacturers but also by many individual ice cream retailers.

Usually bought by people and groups who were celebrating special occasions and holidays, they were available literally in hundreds of categories. Some of the more popular ones were sports oriented, such as football, baseball, and golf. Holidays such as Easter, Christmas, and Thanksgiving were also featured, as were celebrations like weddings, engagements, birthdays, anniversaries and graduations. You could also buy molded ice cream that recognized patriotic events, fraternal orders, and such things as flowers, fruits, and vegetables. In reality, there were well over one thousand different designs that could be ordered to help celebrate and recognize people or things important to the moment. The selling of molded ice cream figures was a significant portion of business for many ice cream makers because public recognition of the special treat for special occasions was enormous.

All of this came to an end about 1965 when the government prohibited the use of pewter ice cream molds in the manufacture of ice cream. The pewter, a combination of tin and lead, often contained as much as 39% lead and it was thought that people would get lead poisoning. And so, many of the commercial ice cream manufacturers simply disposed of their molds, just as they did with any other piece of unusable, extraneous equipment. They were not, in essence, considered to be collectibles back then. By the time an interest developed in them, the number of molds available to collectors had diminished considerably.

Molds came in two sizes: Individual portions and one called a Banquet Mold, which made a dessert that could serve six or more portions. A Philadelphia pewterer by the name of William Will was known to have had pewter ice cream molds in his shop over two hundred years ago.

Molded ice cream Fancy Forms were all handmade specialties. Many of them were colored by the use of different flavored ice creams, such as vanilla, chocolate, strawberry, or pistachio. Sometimes the coloring was achieved by spraying or even dipping the ice cream into a liquid food color. Making Fancy Forms was quite labor intensive. The majority of the ice cream makers who made them issued special sales brochures in the form of booklets. These, too, have become a collectible in their own right.

The two major mold manufacturers in the United States were Eppelsheimer and Company of New York, whose molds were marked "E & Co. N.Y."; and Schall and Company, also of New York and dating back to 1854, who marked their molds "S & Co." The Krauss Company of Milford, Pennsylvania eventually bought out Schall.

In addition to the manufacturer's initials being on the mold, the molds also carried the item number as designated in the maker's catalogs.

There are some molds found occasionally from M. Cadot et Cie of Paris that carry a "CC" mark. However, the general focus here is on American molds.

Collectors of ice cream molds are not vast in number but they are, without exception, a dedicated group who take pride in what they have discovered.

Santa banquet (round base), Krauss (S & Co.). $1,110-1,300.
Santa banquet (square base with folded arms), Epplesheimer & Co. (E & Co.). $1,110-1,300.
Fireplace and Stockings, Epplesheimer & Co. (E&Co.). $250-350.
Christmas Sleigh, Kraus (S & Co.). $150-250.

Large swan (swept wings on pedestal), Cadot et Cie (CC). $800-1,000. Swan swimming with wings folded, Letang. $600-800.

Large train ("John Bull" locomotive), Epplesheimer & Co. (E&Co.). $1,200-1,500. Miscellaneous train, locomotives, and cars, assorted train set, both Epplesheimer & Krauss. $125-200 each.

Large lobster banquet, Letang. $750-800. Small lobster, Krauss (S & Co.). $100-150.

Three children on sleigh banquet, George Leib. $1,200-1,500.

Large heart cupids (open), Epplesheimer (E & Co.). $1,110-1,500.

Large lily, Krauss (S & Co.). $850-1,000. Small lily, Krauss (S & Co). $75-150.

Girl holding basket with birds at feet, Keinke. $750-1,000.

Large heart cupids (closed), Epplesheimer (E & Co.). $1,110-1,500.

Large flower arrangement in urn, Cadot et Cie (CC). $1,000-1,500. Matching small flower arrangement, Cadot et Cie (CC). $75-125.

Owl, George Norman. $800-1,200.

Large flying dove, George Norman. $500-750. Rare "J.B" dove, Julius Boehmer. $750-1,000. Small dove, Epplesheimer & Co. (E & Co.). $100-150.

EASTER
#189 S Rabbit
#297 S & Co. Rabbit
#190 S & Co. Rabbit
#292 S & Co. Chick in egg
#M1198 E & Co. Three chicks on basket
#1005 E & Co. Knight Templar's cross
$75-100 each, with the less common ones in the $150 range

Pineapple banquet, unknown manufacturer. $350-500. Small pineapple, unknown manufacturer. $75-100.

MISCELLANEOUS
#341 S & Co. Noah's ark
#588 S & Co. Tea pot
#973 E & Co. Eiffel Tower
#569 S & Co. Loving cup, three pieces
#1115 E & Co. Kewpie, PAT March 4-13 #43680
$60-175 each

VALENTINE'S DAY
#982 E & Co. Cupid
#492 S Cupid
#583 S Cupid on shell
#300 S & Co. Hearts aflame
#506 S Valentine
$60-125 each

CHRISTMAS
#1154 E & Co. Christmas tree
#1146 E & Co. Wreath
#1144 E & Co. Poinsettia
#991 E & Co. Santa Claus
#427 S Santa Claus
$100-200 each

ANIMALS
#271 S & Co. Horse and jockey
#579 S & Co. Horse head
#677 E & Co. Dove
#179 S Fox
#835 BIS CC Bird
$60-125 each with the more unusual ones in the $175 range

ANIMALS
#X-32 Unmarked swan
#181 S Butterfly
$60-125 each, with the more unusual ones in the $175 range

THANKSGIVING
#270 S & Co. Corn
#1004 E & Co. Horn of Plenty
#M1208 E & Co. Pilgrim boy with blunderbuss
#650 E & Co. Turkey
$50-100 each, with the more unusual one in the
$150-200 range

PINEAPPLES
#14 S & Co. Large Pineapple banquet
#xx Harton & Son Hinged Pineapple banquet, London
#156 S & Co. Pineapple, tallest of individual sized
#253 E & Co. Pineapple, next to tallest of individual sized
#129 E & Co. Pineapple
#xxx Unmarked Pineapple, no design on outside
#1697 LG Pineapple, smallest
#99 Unmarked Pineapple, medallion
$50-85 each; banquet size $400-500 each

SPORTS
#622 Krauss Son Golf bag
#1048 E & Co. Golf ball
#463 S Male golfer
$75-150 each

FLOWERS
#349 S Gladiolus
#582 S American Beauty rose
#209 S Pond lily
#316 S & Co. Sunflower
$50-75 each

HALLOWEEN
#1180 E Cat and moon
#1153 (E) NY Witch Riding broom
#M 1207 E & Co. Witch head
#E1206 E & Co. Jack O'Lantern
#M1205 E & Co. Pumpkin and Corn, Jack O'Lantern
$100-175 each, with the most unusual ones in the $175-250 range

PATRIOTIC
#1160 E & Co. American Flag
#2000 E & Co. Flag over Capital
#1073 E Uncle Sam
#283 S & Co. American Eagle
$100-150 each, with the less common ones in the $150-200 range

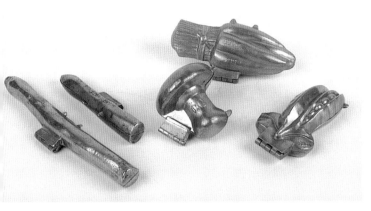

VEGETABLES
#X2 Unmarked Asparagus
#814 BIS CC Mushroom
#305 S & Co. Bunch of Carrots
#293 S & Co. Pea Pod
#498 S & Co. Asparagus
$35-50 each

VEGETABLES
Open molds showing interior

TRANSPORTATION
#472 S Locomotive
#478 S & Co. Coal tender
#479 S & Co. Railroad coach
$75-150 each

TRANSPORTATION
#623 Krauss automobile
#431 S Bicycle, lady riding
#551 S & Co. Bicycle, man riding
#1132 E & Co. Airplane
#553 S & Co. Sailboat
$75-150 each

AQUATIC
#258 S & Co. Dolphin
#184 S & Co. Turtle
#330 S Lobster
#185 S & Co. Fish
#xxx Unmarked Small Fish
$50-75 each

Chapter 11
Straw Holders

The U. S. Patent Office credits Marvin Stone for the invention of the paper drinking straw during early 1888. Prior to this invention, the stalk of the natural Rye plant was harvested, trimmed, and used as a drinking straw.

The late author and respected glass researcher, William Heacock, reported that a July 19, 1888 glass manufacturing trade journal contained an announcement proclaiming the production and availability of a "fancy" glass straw jar. The jar has been determined to be the "Chrysanthemum Swirl" pattern that was produced by the Northwood Glass Company at the direction of Harry Northwood. This announcement remains the earliest confirmed existence of a glass soda fountain "straw jar." The earliest documented evidence of a metal straw holder was found in the *American Soda Book* dating to the late 1880s.

Because of a lack of reference material, there are few absolutes in this general discussion on straw holders, and although there may well be exceptions to what is stated, there is no intention to mislead. But there is one thing for certain, and that is that the straw holder is an integral part of soda fountain history.

Examples of the earliest known straw jars were produced during the Victorian Era. They remain to this time as extremely beautiful yet fragile examples of handcrafted Victorian glass. Early jars almost universally were produced with matching glass covers. While most covers had finials (knobs), two of the earliest known examples were actually made without finials. Not many jars were produced and far fewer survived the rigors of use by both the soda fountain employees and the public. Due to handling, the covers remained most vulnerable to breakage, and were often destroyed when dropped onto the "old" marble countertop. As such, complete jars are rare and highly cherished by collectors today.

Some of the earliest jars have opalescent white "candy cane" stripes. These stripes were not painted, but instead, were created by a complex patented process that involved heating, molding, re-heating, and re-molding a special glass formula. Other jars were ornately decorated with fired enamel paintings that were laboriously hand applied. Still other jars were shaped into inverted thumbprint, polka dot, quilt, and ribbed patterns.

As the industrial revolution progressed, so did development of the straw jar. The process of hand blowing and hand decorating survived for over two decades, but ultimately succumbed to the more economical manu-facturing process used to produce pressed pattern glass. In America, pattern glass had become an inexpensive and fashionable substitute for cut glass. It was produced in large quantities during the mid and late nineteenth century. Pattern glass could be produced in extremely ornate patterns, and it was not surprising that pressed pattern glass straw jars evolved in the late 1890s. Pressed glass manufactured prior to World War I is commonly referred to by collectors as "Early American Pattern Glass" (E.A.P.G.). Straw jars were produced with thick molded wall sections that proved far more durable in use than the fragile Victorian Art Glass jars. Pattern glass jars continued to be made with glass covers into the mid 1920s.

Heisey and McKee manufactured horizontal pressed pattern glass straw holders. The term "straw holder" rather than "straw jar" is first observed in the McKee glass catalog description for the horizontal "Colonial Sanitary Straw Holder." Collectors now consider these two terms as synonymous.

Oddly, a similar characteristic of both the Victorian and pattern glass straw jars dramatically contributed to their demise. During the early 1900s, the public became increasingly aware of the impact of microbes to human health. Sanitation became a paramount concern! The horizontal straw holder was designed in part as an early attempt to improve sanitation. These jars were shaped to prevent the user from touching the straw ends, however adjacent straws could still be contaminated as the user picked up a straw in the middle. The horizontal glass straw holder was not "long lived."

In 1912, a combination glass base with a metal lid and insert was patented; it was a revolution in straw jar design and remains in use to this day. Some collectors refer to this type of jar as "Depression Style." The combination holder provided significant improvement with regard to the concerns of sanitation and durability. This holder was sometimes promoted as a "combination straw jar and automatic dispenser." At this point, the purpose of the holder was not only that of containing the straws, it had acquired a secondary purpose of protecting the straws as well. In general, the insert consisted of a nickel-plated metal lid or cover, with a knob on top and a shaft, which was attached to a cup that held the straws. Lifting the lid would raise the straw filled cup and allow the straws to be distributed into a fan shaped pattern. Individual straws could then be dispensed without contamination of adjacent straws. When closed, the straws would remain covered and protected from flies, dust, or other contaminates. By far the most popular pattern for the base was the "Colonial" pattern. Many manufactures varied the design, but maintained the heavy glass pattern with eight, ten, or twelve panels together with the wide base for stability. The glass jars were often manufactured by one company and the metal lid/inserts by another. However, the manufacturer is attributed to the signing on the metal insert, catalog identification, advertising documentation, or by reference books.

Beginning in 1912 and continuing through the teens and 1920s, the jar inserts had a high dome nickel plated brass lid and knob. Later, the domes were lowered, and starting in the 1930s, Bakelite knobs began replacing the metal knobs on the nickel plated lids. Over the decades, the lids were produced with painted or chrome plated covers together with wood, plastic, or metal knobs.

Several innovative modifications appeared over the years to the combination style that allowed the controlled dispensing of one, two, or three straws at a time. Today, collectors refer to one of these jars as the "one, two, three, jar." The No-Touch and Sav-Stras holders also had a unique method of dispensing straws. Several colorful Depression-type jars were produced in green, amber, blue, red, orange, and yellow with inserts painted the same color as the jar.

Although the vertical, all glass Victorian jars were initially the most decorative and popular straw holders, both vertical and horizontal holders in glass and metal were being offered by the American Soda Fountain Company as early as the late 1880s. Later, horizontal holders were being manufactured of aluminum, iron, or steel with chromium, nickel, or silver plating. The Benedict Manufacturing Company started offering all metal vertical holders in the early 1900s. All metal horizontal holders worked on the same principle of pushing a lever to dispense the straw, with the advantage of dispensing only one straw at a time. After 1940, most horizontals quit using the lever and relied on gravity to dispense the straws.

Both glass and metal straw holders provided companies with a convenient place to advertise. A quality advertising straw holder is extremely scarce. Advertising was used on straw holders as early as 1911 by the Hires Company. The soft drink company, Pepsi, had an early square holder produced in metal with their logo, and later holders produced in ceramic. Welch's Grape Juice had at least two different types of early metal holders manufactured. A company that produced a drink called "Grape Smash" had a heavy glass jar with a hinged lid manufactured in the 1920s or 30s. There were many different ice cream and soft drink advertisers on the Rex Aluminum straw holders manufactured in the 1930s and 40s.

Today we see a proliferation of "reproduction" and "fantasy" straw jars primarily intended for home use. They provide an aura of "days gone by" and are enjoyed by many, who, due to the scarcity of valid old straw holders, might otherwise never experience the pleasure of dispensing a drinking straw. A disturbing trend has surfaced to represent fantasy and reproduction straw jars as old collectibles in attempt to capitalize on the value of valid old straw jars. In other instances, vases are misrepresented as straw holders; improper covers are incorrectly married to valid straw jar bases; or barbershop comb holders are misrepresented as valid straw holders. Pillar vases (cylinder vases) were produced during the Victorian era and have very similar characteristics to straw jars. These vases are quite beautiful, however they were never produced with a cover. Sometimes there is even a decorative bulbous ring located below the top similar to a straw jar. A pillar vase can be distinguished from a straw jar by a bulbous ring that is either missing or located too far down the neck of the bottle to support a normal straw jar cover. Many antique and collectable categories are blighted by deceit.

Victorian blown opalescent pattern glass, possibly manufactured by the American Glass Co. or the Buckeye Glass Co., c. beginning in 1889. Pattern is "Reverse Swirl" (Ribbed Pillar). The Reverse Swirl is one of the three known Victorian opalescent patterns produced as a straw jar. It is considered to be one of the earlier jars manufactured. Characteristics of this blue swirl jar include a ground glass lip on the base and cover together with an applied finial (knob). Known in cranberry swirl and flint swirl; also known in both glossy and satin finishes. $5,500-6,500.

The value estimates included in the descriptions are based on straw holders in complete and undamaged condition. It becomes a very complex issue to further discuss values of holders with missing or incorrect tops, glass damage, or manufacturing flaws. Other problems to be considered include dented metal covers, corrosion or worn plating, damaged or missing decals, incorrect inserts, or missing parts. These conditions can impact value to a greater or lesser degree. The actual value becomes the agreed value established from a sales transaction by both a knowledgeable buyer and seller. Some of the earlier straw holders are so rare that sometimes only one or two examples are known to exist. Since these unique items are seldom offered for sale, little information is available about valuations.

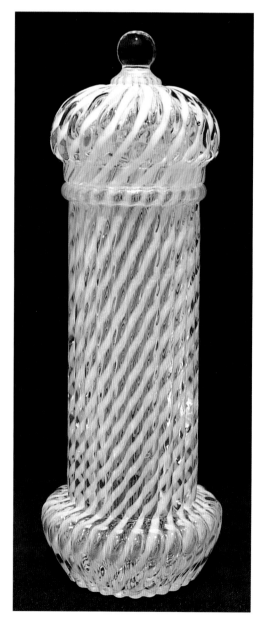

Victorian blown opalescent pattern glass, manufactured by the Northwood Glass Co., c. beginning in 1888. Pattern is "Chrysanthemum Swirl" (Ribbed Pillar). The Chrysanthemum Swirl is considered the earliest straw jar style produced. Characteristics of this blue swirl jar include a ground glass lip on the base and cover together with an applied finial (knob). Known in cranberry swirl and flint swirl; also known in both glossy and satin finishes. $5,500-6,500.

Victorian blown opalescent pattern glass, manufactured by the Northwood Glass Co., c. beginning in 1888. Pattern is "Chrysanthemum Swirl" (Ribbed Pillar). The Chrysanthemum Swirl is considered the earliest straw jar style produced. Characteristics of this flint swirl jar include a ground glass lip on the base and cover together with an applied finial (knob). Known in blue swirl and cranberry swirl; also known in both glossy and satin finishes. $5,000-6,000.

Victorian blown opalescent pattern glass, manufactured by the Northwood Glass Co., c. beginning in 1888. Pattern is "Chrysanthemum Swirl" (Ribbed Pillar). The Chrysanthemum Swirl is considered the earliest straw jar style produced. Characteristics of this cranberry swirl jar include a ground glass lip on the base and cover together with an applied finial (knob). Known in blue swirl and flint swirl; also known in both glossy and satin finishes. This jar is missing a cover. $5,500-6,500 (complete jar with correct cover).

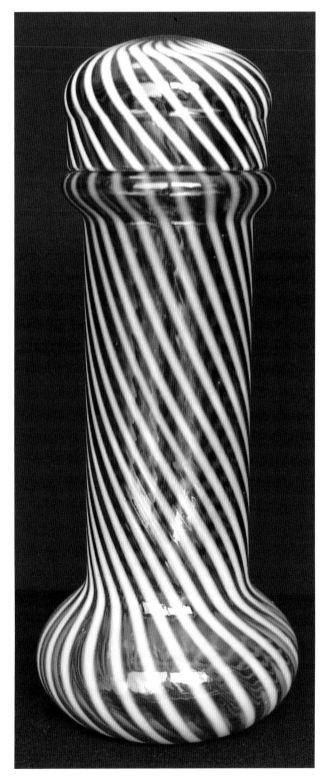

Victorian blown opalescent pattern glass, possibly manufactured by the Hobbs Glass Co. or Northwood Glass Co., c. 1889-1904. Pattern is "Opalescent Swirl." The Opalescent Swirl with bulbous base is one of the three known Victorian opalescent patterns produced as a straw jar. It is considered one of the earlier jars manufactured. Characteristics of this cranberry swirl jar include a ground glass lip on the base and cover. Known in blue swirl and flint swirl; also known in both glossy and satin finishes. It was produced without a finial (knob). $5,000-6,000.

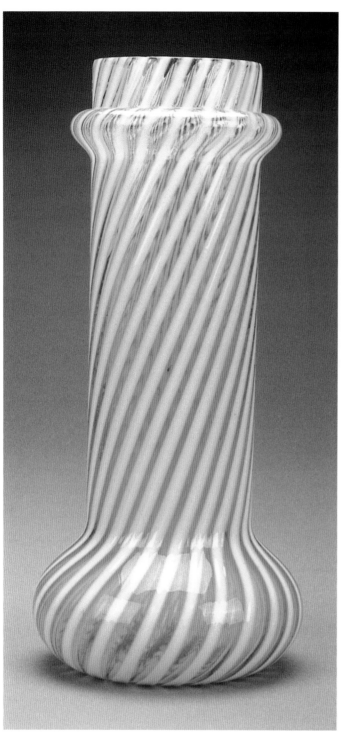

Victorian blown pattern glass, unknown manufacturer, c. 1890-1900. Pattern is "Polka Dot." Peacock blue Polka Dot bulbous base; glass lid produced without a finial (knob); ground glass lip on base and cover; known also in cranberry. $3,500-4000.

Victorian blown opalescent pattern glass, possibly manufactured by the Hobbs Glass Co. or Northwood Glass Co., c. 1889-1904. Pattern is "Opalescent Swirl." The Opalescent Swirl with bulbous base is one of the three known Victorian opalescent patterns produced as a straw jar. It is considered one of the earlier jars manufactured. Characteristics of this blue swirl jar include a ground glass lip on the base and cover. Known in cranberry swirl and flint swirl; also known in both glossy and satin finishes. It was produced without a finial (knob). $5,000-6000 (complete jar with correct cover).

Victorian blown pattern glass, unknown manufacturer, c. 1890-1900. Pattern is Inverted Thumbprint. Cranberry Inverted Thumbprint with bulbous base; ground glass lip on base and lid; feather of cranberry in the crystal finial (knob). $4,000-4,500.

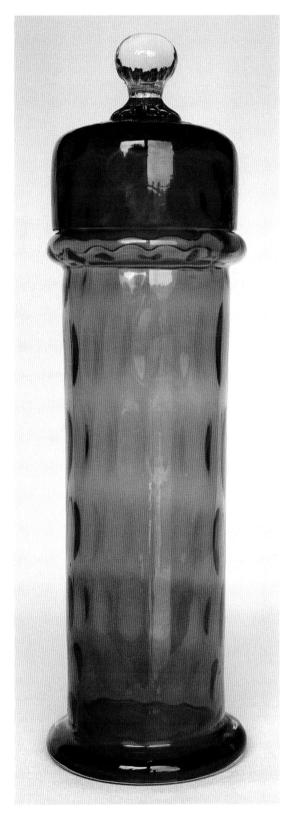

Victorian blown pattern glass, unknown manufacturer, c. 1890-1900. Pattern is Inverted Thumbprint. Cranberry Inverted Thumbprint; ground glass lip on base and lid; and applied finial (knob). $3,500-4000.

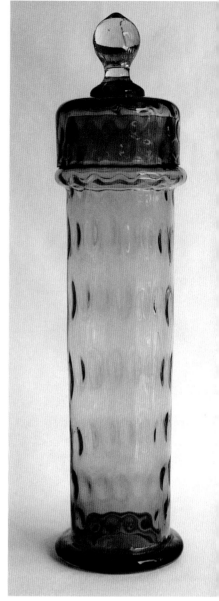

Victorian blown pattern glass, unknown manufacturer, c. 1895-1905. Pattern is Inverted
Thumbprint. Tall cranberry Inverted Thumbprint;
ground glass lip on base and lid; base height is
identical to base height of the tall Depression
style colonial jar. $3,500-4,000.

Victorian blown pattern glass, unknown manufacturer, c. 1890-1905. Pattern is Inverted Thumbprint. The jars are crystal, peacock blue, and amber; bulbous base; known also in cranberry. A
version of this jar is known to have a cover with a flattened finial (knob). $2,500-3000 each
(complete jar with correct cover).

Victorian blown pattern glass, unknown manufacturer, c. 1890-1905. Pattern is Vertical Interior Ribs. Cranberry bulbous base with vertical interior ribs; polished pontil; applied "Rose Bud" finial (knob) on cover; ground glass lip on cover. $3,000-3,500.

Victorian blown pattern glass, unknown manufacturer, c. 1890-1900. Pattern is "Quilt." Vaseline Quilt pattern; ground glass lip on base; cover cast in triple piece mold. $3,500-4,000.

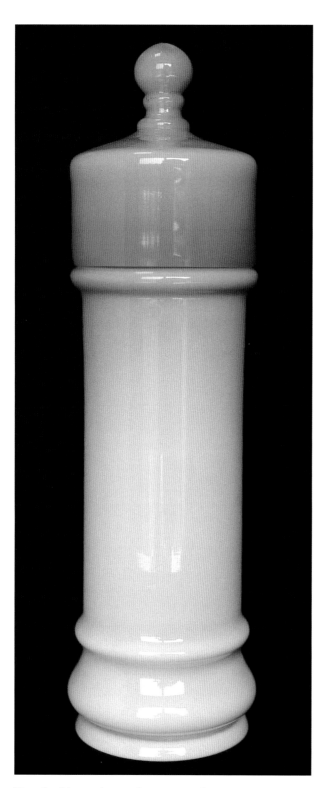

Victorian blown pattern glass, unknown manufacturer, c. 1890-1905. Pattern is Vertical Interior Ribs. Amber glass; gold and white fired enamel hand painted decoration; ground glass lip on base and cover; possibly decorated by the Beaumont Glass Co. $4,000-4,500.

Victorian blown glass, unknown manufacturer, c. 1890-1900. Pink cased glass; appears similar to "Peachblow"; ground glass lip on base and lid; color transitions from raspberry to light pink. $4,000-4,500.

Victorian blown pattern glass, unknown manufacturer, c. 1895-1905. Pattern is Vertical Interior Ribs. Rubina glass; fired enamel hand painting; ground glass lip on base and lid; known also in both cranberry and blue glass. $5,500-6,000.

Victorian blown glass, unknown manufacturer, date unknown. Green Coca-Cola decorated; fired enamel hand painting; blown bulbous base with ground glass lip; metal lid; decoration also known on straight sided cranberry jar. $5,000-5,500.

Victorian blown glass, manufactured by the McKee Glass Co., c. 1904-1910. Blue straw jar with fired enamel hand painted decoration; ground glass lip on base; known also in green glass; possibly decorated by the Beaumont Glass Co. $3,000-3,500.

Victorian blown glass, unknown manufacturer, c. 1898-1905. Cranberry "Have a Soft Drink" straw jar with missing lid; fired enamel hand painted decoration; known also in green glass. $4,500-5,000 (complete jar with correct cover).

E.A.P.G., unknown manufacturer, c. 1900-1910. Pattern is Colonial. Paneled white milk glass; footed base; bulbous glass lid. $1,800-2,300.

Victorian blown pattern glass, unknown manufacturer, c. 1895-1905. Bulbous base with cut glass decoration; cut glass lid; cut glass faceted finial (knob); ground glass lip on lid; polished pontil. $1,800-2,300.

Victorian blown glass, unknown manufacturer,
c. Depression era. This holder has a vertical rib pattern
in the base and lid. $800-1,000.

Victorian blown glass, unknown manufacturer, c. Depression era. Heavy glass base with thick wall. $800-1,000.

E.A.P.G., manufactured by the U.S. Glass Co., c. 1902-1915. Pattern is "Manhattan." Advertised as available with a glass lid, silver-plated metal lid, or a silver-plated metal-banded rim. $1,000-1,200.

E.A.P.G., manufactured by the U.S. Glass Co., c. 1902-1915. Pattern is "Manhattan." Decorated with gold gilding and maiden's blush flashing on both the base and glass lid. $3,000-3,500.

E.A.P.G., manufac-
tured by the U.S.
Glass Co., c. 1897-
1921. Pattern is
"Illinois." The
manufacturer
distributed the straw
jar with and without a
lid. The base was
also advertised as a
vase. The manufac-
turer also used the
base as the bottom of
an oil lamp. The jar is
known to be deco-
rated with gold
gilding and ruby
flashing on both the
base and lid.
$600-800.

E.A.P.G., manufactured by the U.S. Glass Co., c. 1897-
1921. Pattern is "Illinois." Produced in a limited quantity
of emerald green glass with and without gold gilding.
$2,000-2,500.

E.A.P.G., manufactured by the U.S. Glass Co., c. 1897-1921. Pattern is "Illinois." The "Scalloped" foot is possibly from an early generation mold used to produce the straw jar. $1,800-2,300.

E.A.P.G., manufactured by the U.S. Glass Co., c. beginning in 1899. Pattern is Bohemian (also known as the "Flora Dora" pattern). This example is missing the lid. Known also in rose flashed (maiden's blush), green, crystal, and frosted crystal, all of which have gold gilding. $3,500-4,000 (rose flashed, maiden blush glass w/lid); $3,500-4,000 (green glass w/lid); $2,800-3,300 (crystal glass w/lid); $3,000-3,500 (frosted glass w/lid).

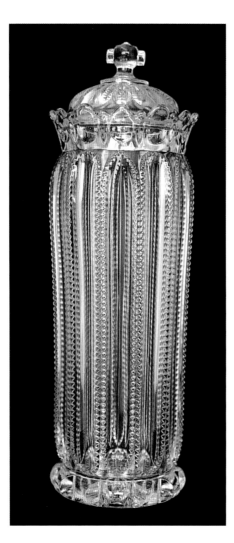

E.A.P.G., manufactured by the McKee Glass Co., c. 1904-1910. Pattern is "Prize." Known also with gold gilding and ruby stain. $1,000-1,200 (crystal w/glass lid); $3,000-3,500 (w/ gold gilding, ruby stain, and w/glass lid).

E.A.P.G., manufactured by the U.S. Glass Co., c. 1908-1926. Colonial pattern #3989 advertised in a 1926 soda fountain trade journal as dust proof and fly proof for sixty cents. $700-900.

E.A.P.G., manufactured by the McKee Glass Co., c. 1904-1927. Pattern is Colonial. Bulbous glass lid. $800-1,000.

E.A.P.G., unknown manufacturer, c. 1898-1908. Pattern resembles the Fostoria "Edgewood" pattern. The pattern is sometimes referred to as the "Zipper" pattern. The jar was produced with a silver-plated metal cover. $1,500-2,000 (complete jar with correct cover).

E.A.P.G., manufactured by the McKee Glass Co., c. 1904-1927. Pattern is "Aztec." Glass cover has same pattern as base. Signed "Pres Cut" on bottom. $1,500-2,000 (complete jar with correct cover).

E.A.P.G., manufactured by the A. H. Heisey & Co., c. 1906-1911. Patterns are Colonial and "Greek Key." Five short individual jars. All jars are signed with the Heisey Diamond "H" trademark. $100-250 each.

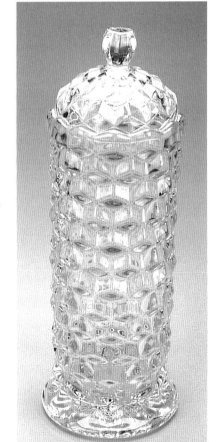

E.A.P.G., manufactured by the Fostoria Glass Co., c. 1915-1924. Pattern is "American." $400-500.

E.A.P.G., manufactured by the A. H. Heisey & Co., c. 1905-1920. Patterns are Colonial, "Prison Stripe," and "Greek Key" (left to right). Three regular size jars. All jars are signed with the Heisey Diamond "H" trademark. A sugar jar lid is sometimes incorrectly used on the Colonial and Greek Key jars. The correct Colonial and Greek Key lid has eight panels. The Greek Key lid sleeves over the glass bottom in a "mushroom-like" fashion. The lids as shown have ten panels. $1,000-1,500 each (complete jar with correct cover).

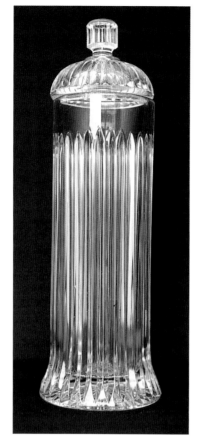

E.A.P.G., unknown manufacturer, c. date unknown. Advertised in an undated soda fountain trade journal with picture. $700-900.

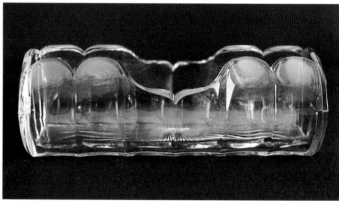

E.A.P.G. Horizontal, manufactured by the A.H. Heisey & Co., c. 1905-1911. Pattern is Colonial. Marked with the Heisey Diamond "H" trademark. $700-900.

E.A.P.G. Horizontal, manufactured by the McKee Glass Co., c. 1904-1927. Pattern is "Toltec." Advertised by manufacturer as "Flat" Toltec Sanitary Straw Jar. $700-900.

Advertising horizontal, manufactured by the Jersey Crème Co., c. early 1900s. The base is E.A.P.G. with a metal top. Known as the Jersey Crème dispenser. "Roof" at top lifts to gain access to straws. $3,500-4000.

Advertising horizontals, unknown manufacturer, c. beginning in 1911. Both holders are made of cast iron. The holder on the left is known as the Hires Root Beer dispenser. It is signed on the inside with "Loaned by the Charles E. Hires Co." The holder on the right will dispense straws in front and back whereas the Hires only dispenses in the front. Coincidentally, both holders contain the same patent dates of Oct. 24, 1911 and Nov. 14, 1911. $4,000-5,000 (left); $500-800 (right).

Advertising horizontal, manufactured by the Rex Mfg. Co., c. 1930s-1940s. The drum is made of aluminum. Soft drink and ice cream manufacturers advertised on these models. Straw release levers are located on both ends. One end of the unit is removed to replace straws. $600-800 each.

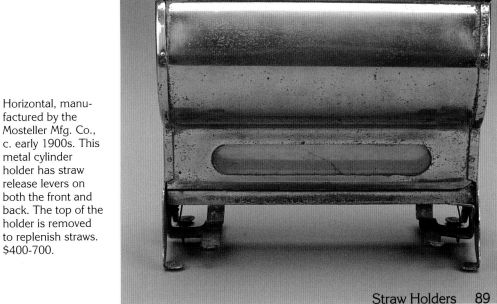

Advertising, manufactured by the Cleveland Fruit Juice Co., c. 1920s. Pattern is Colonial. The base is pressed glass. The complete holder has a unique hinged metal lid. The company initials "CJ" appear on both sides of the jar together with the advertisement. The advertisement on the jar contains the words, "Drink Grape Smash." $4,000-4,500 (complete jar with correct cover).

Horizontal, manufactured by the Mosteller Mfg. Co., c. early 1900s. This metal cylinder holder has straw release levers on both the front and back. The top of the holder is removed to replenish straws. $400-700.

Horizontal, manufactured by the Shupp's Woodwork Co., c. beginning in 1959. Straw release levers are located on both ends of this wooden holder. Straws were replenished through the back. $50-100.

Horizontal, manufactured by the Monarch Straw Dispenser Co., c. beginning in 1912. This metal holder has straw release levers located on both the front and back. The top was removed to replenish the straws. $400-700.

Horizontal, manufactured by the Miller's Sanitary Straw Dispenser Co., c. beginning in 1939. This chrome plated holder has a straw release lever located on the right side. The top was removed to replenish the straws. Dispenser was well constructed. $300-400.

All metal, manufactured by the American Soda Fountain Co., c. beginning in 1888. This holder was silver plated. One of the oldest all-metal and one of the first documented straw holders. $800-1,000.

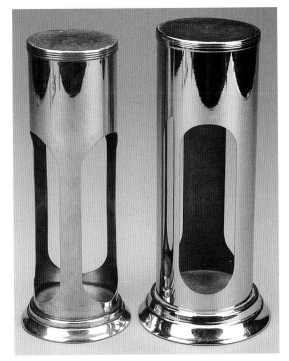

All metal, manu-
factured by the
Benedict Mfg. Co.,
c. beginning in
1927. Made of
heavy gauge drawn
seamless tubing,
nickel plated and
then heavily silver
plated. $50-100
each.

All metal, manufactured by the Benedict Mfg. Co.,
c. beginning in 1915 (left); Cecilware, c. 1930s (center);
Maryland Products Co., c. beginning 1940 (right). The
Benedict model is silver plated, Cecilware is 18% nickel
silver, and the Pepsi Cola holder is chrome plated. $50
(left); $50-75 (center); $300 (right).

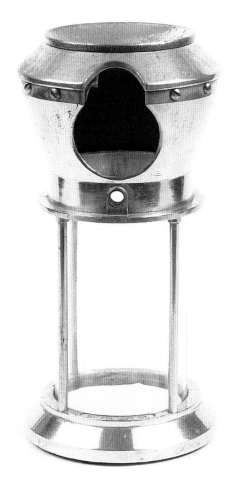

Combination glass and
metal, manufactured by the
Wilton Mfg. Co.,
c. beginning in 1913. The
complete unit has a
mechanism that dispenses a
straw through the opening
by turning a knob. The
holder turns on a ball-
bearing base and was well
made. It compares in weight
to the cast iron horizontal
straw holders. Most units
seen today have the knob
and mechanism removed,
leaving an opening through
which the straws were
accessed. Referred to as
"Sav-Stras Straw Dispenser"
in the advertisements.
$800-1,000 (complete unit).

Combination glass with metal lid and insert, unknown
manufacturer, c. 1912-1938. Jars are mold-blown and are
identical except one has extra heavy glass at base. The
insert was designed to be removed and passed around the
table. Some advertisements called these straw holders the
"Florence Automatic Glass Straw Dispenser." The earliest
model has 1912-1916 patent dates stamped into the nickel
plated lid. $200-400 cach.

Combination glass with metal lid and insert, manufactured by the No-Touch Straw Holder Co., c. beginning in 1917. Pattern is Colonial. The base is pressed glass and the cover and insert rod are aluminum. The original jar was only made in crystal. The insert rod has a fish hook on the end to pull up one straw at a time through the hole in the lid. This jar is signed on the bottom with the manufacturer name, the patent date, and the name "Sani-"Straw." This holder has been recently reproduced in cobalt, green, pink, and crystal. The sign lettering on the bottom of the reproduced jars is blurry and not sharp. There are also original jars with reproduced aluminum lids and insert rods. The original insert rod and knob have threads while the reproduced insert rod and knob are one-piece. $250-400 (as originally produced in crystal).

Combination glass with metal lid and insert, unknown manufacturer, c. 1920s. Pattern is Colonial. Jar is mold-blown. The high insert base prevents straws from falling out as they are raised. $200-350.

Combination glass with metal lid and insert, unknown manufacturer, c. 1918-1926. Pattern is Colonial. Jar is pressed glass and dispenses one, two, or three straws which gave it the name "one-two-three." $300-400.

Combination glass with metal lid and insert, unknown manufacturer, c. 1915-1930. Pattern is Colonial with chain design. Jars are pressed glass. Shown in crystal and green. The jar has been recently reproduced in cobalt, green, milk glass, ice blue, and pink. At this time, the reproduction jar is always missing the nickel plated screw-on base. The original nickel plated base will not fit on the screw threads of the reproduced jar. $200-400 (crystal); $800-900 (green).

Combination glass with metal lid and insert, unknown manufacturer, c. 1920s. Jars are pressed glass. Both holders must have been produced by the same company. They are unusual in that they both have springs attached to the bottom of the cup. The purpose of the springs is to slow the lifting of the cup. $150-250 (regular size jar); $800-1,000 (wide size jar).

Combination glass with metal lid and insert, unknown manufacturer, c. 1912-1920s. Pattern is Colonial. Jars are pressed glass. The tinted glass resulted from an exposure to sunlight. The clear crystal jar is signed "Florence" on the bottom. $125-200 (tinted unsigned); $200-400 (signed "Florence").

Combination glass with metal lid and insert, unknown manufacturer, c. 1920s. Pattern is Colonial. Jars are pressed glass. These two holders used a different method of stopping the insert from being pulled out by careless customers. The one with the button stop resembles a "Gilchrist Sanitary Glass Straw Dispenser" advertised in a 1926 catalog. $125-200 (button stop glued on side); $200-300 (metal ring stopper).

Combination glass with metal lid and insert, unknown manufacturer, c. 1930s. Pattern is Colonial. Jars are pressed glass and taller than normal size jars. Insert shafts are hinged in the style manufactured by the Benedict Mfg. Co. $150-250 (crystal); $400-700 (green).

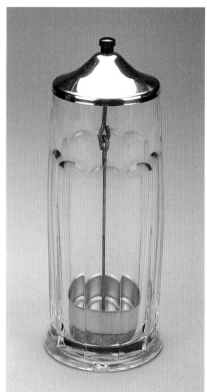

Combination glass with metal lid and insert, manufactured by the Benedict Mfg. Co., c. 1930s. Pattern is Colonial. Jars are pressed glass. Menu holder attached to the crystal jar. $125-200 (crystal); $300-500 (green).

Combination glass with metal lid and insert, manufactured by the Benedict Mfg. Co., c. 1930s. Pattern is Colonial. Jar is pressed glass and has a unique barrel shape and is referred to by collectors as the "Barrel Jar." The insert cup is signed and the insert shaft is hinged. The jar is known in crystal and green. $300-400.

Combination glass with metal lid and insert, manufactured by the Benedict Mfg. Co., c. 1930s. Pattern is Colonial. The jar is pressed glass; has a unique barrel shape; and is referred to by collectors as the "Barrel Jar." The insert cup is signed, and the insert shaft is hinged. The jar is known in crystal and green. $500-700.

Combination glass with metal lid and insert, manufactured by the Hamilton Beach Co., c. 1930s. Pattern is Colonial. Jar is pressed glass and not signed, but is exactly like a holder advertised in a 1933 *Soda Fountain Magazine* as a Hamilton Beach Straw Dispenser with the green Bakelite knob on lid. This jar could be purchased with a rubber base protector. The jar is known in crystal and green. $125-200.

Combination glass with metal lid and insert, unknown manufacturer, c. 1930s. Pattern is Colonial. Jar is pressed glass and etched with a wheat and flower design. $250-300.

Combination glass with metal lid and insert, unknown manufacturer, c. 1950s-1960s. Colored glass with painted metal lid and insert together with a matching painted wooden knob. Known only in red, yellow, orange, green, and blue colors. $200-300 each.

Combination glass with metal lid and insert and an all metal with insert, manufactured by the Star Straw Dispensers Co., c. 1930s-1940s. Inserts are identical. Jar was mold-blown, and the panels are convex. The glass version has been seen with an insert cup that has holes. Barber shop "comb holders" have holes in the insert cup to drain sterilizing fluid. Comb holders are not considered as straw holders! $150-250.

Combination glass with metal lid and insert, unknown manufacturer, c. Depression era. The jars are plain mold-blown. Shown in green and amber. $200-300 each.

Chapter 12
Ice Cream Fountain Ware

This is also a soda fountain collectible with an infinite number of items to generate interest. Metal or glass, the choices are there. The primary focus is on sundae dishes and banana split dishes with a variety of styles and shapes. There is an equally large selection of ice cream soda glasses, which are fun to find.

Cecileware metal sundae dishes $35 each.

Glass cone holder, $45.

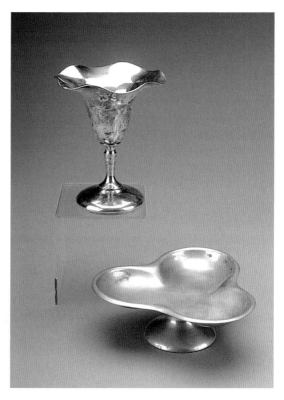

Indestructo metal sundae dishes. $35-40 each.

Footed banana split dishes: Heisey clear, $40; Heisey plain, $25; Heisey amber, Sahara Pattern, $100; Heisey green, $45.

Double scoop dish. Green, $75; clear, $35.

Soda glasses. Plain and green, $50; Lucky Mondae glass, $75-85.

Fired on soda glasses, $35 each.

Fired on sundae dishes, $35 each.

Sundae dishes. Pink and green, $45 each; plain with flared up sides, $35.

Chapter 13
The Milkshake Machine

The old soda fountain contributed four "S's" to our culture: the ice cream **S**undae, the banana **S**plit, the ice cream **S**oda and the milk **S**hake. In a sense, they have all endured—the shake perhaps better than most because it remains a standard menu choice at nearly every fast food chain today.

When William Horlick, of Racine, Wisconsin, began marketing dry milk and malt powder in 1887, two things were immediately apparent. One, that people liked the taste of the malt powder mixed with milk; and two, that getting the powder to dissolve in the milk was a difficult and tedious task. Nevertheless, malted milk drinks became a popular choice at the soda fountain counter.

Initial attempts to vigorously shake the malt and the milk together by using a hand shaker made the druggists running the soda fountains nervous, lest their establishments be confused with a common saloon. As a result, soda fountain equipment companies began offering several different hand-cranked mechanical mixers to do the job.

In 1897, *The Standard Manual of Soda and Other Beverages* listed the following recipe for a Milk Shake:

> Put about 4 ounces of shaved ice into a thick 12-ounce glass; add 1 fluid ounce of vanilla syrup, fill glass with milk, and agitate the whole thoroughly. The shaking can be done in a special machine known as a "milk shaker," or by means of a small hand shaker like that used for making egg drinks. Then strain into another glass and serve. Shake on some powdered nutmeg if desired.

As you can see, original milkshakes had no ice cream in them. However, some fountain operators tried incorporating ice cream. Their customers considered this a novel idea and it received quick acceptance, then rapidly lost its appeal. It wasn't until about 1915 that public demand for the milkshake with ice cream caught fire again,

and this combination went on to become the standard fountain drink we are familiar with today.

In 1910, Chester Beach, an employee of the Standard Electric Co., also, in Racine, Wisconsin, developed the fractional horsepower Universal Motor. This compact device could run on AC or DC and could be used to power a number of home appliances, such as sewing machines, floor polishers, and, of course, drink mixers. Fred Osius, president of Standard Electric Co., paid Chester Beach, and another employee, Louis Hamilton, $1,000 each to use their names, forming the Hamilton-Beach Manufacturing Co. in 1912.

Hamilton-Beach Manufacturing Co. subsequently developed the Cyclone mixer, which used the Universal Motor—mounted vertically—to mix and aerate the drink in the cup. Initial models pushed the motor shaft down into the cup, which also started the mixing action. The next models used hanging cups, with the weight of the drink activating the motor switch. The mechanism then progressed to the current configuration, in which pushing the cup under a lip starts the motor running.

As the milkshake evolved to include ice cream, more power was needed to mix the drink. Motor bearings went from sleeve bearings requiring regular oiling to sealed ball bearings. Most of these durable commercial mixers from the 1940s made by Hamilton-Beach, Oster, and Myers are still running strong today.

The designs of these mixers closely followed the design trends of the time: plain white porcelain in the 1920s, Art Deco designs in the 1930s, and bright vibrant colors in the 1940s and 1950s. Unfortunately, machines from the 1960s on are usually stark and utilitarian, although some new machines are starting to have a "retro" look, harking back to those good old days.

As collectibles, the rarity of the milkshake machines shown here is indicated by numbers varying from 5 down to 1, with 5 being the more difficult to find.

Opposite page:
Table Top Mechanical, Coles Mfg. Co. (without tops), Philadelphia, Pennsylvania, c. 1900. 22"-24", black, hand cranked. Rarity 5, $800-1,400.

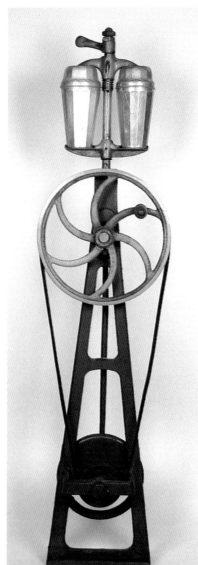

Floor Model Mechanical, Quick and Easy Co., Pittsburgh, Pennsylvania, c. 1900. 48" x 50", red, hand cranked. Rarity 5, $800-1,400

Kwik Mix Mechanical, Kwik Mix Mfg., c. 1900. 10-1/2" x 15", metal with wood base, hand cranked. Rarity 4, $200-600.

Kraft Malted Milk Mixer (left), A.C. Gilbert Co., New Haven Connecticut, c. 1935. 12-1/2", green, sleeve bearing. Rarity 3, $75-125.
Thompsons Malted Milk Mixer (right), A.C. Gilbert Co., New Haven, Connecticut, c. 1935. 9", gray, sleeve bearing. Rarity 3, $75-125.

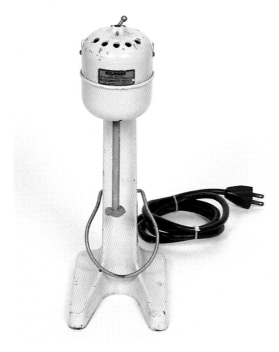

Gilbert, A.C. Gilbert Co., New Haven, Connecticut, c. 1940. 12-1/2", beige, sleeve bearing. Rarity 3, $75-100.

Model 11, Arnold Electric Co., Racine, Wisconsin, c. 1914. 14", white, sleeve bearing. Rarity 3, $125-150.

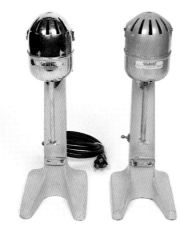

Model B2, A.C. Gilbert Co., New Haven, Connecticut, c. 1945. 12-1/2", green, sleeve bearing. Rarity 1, $40-75.

Model 15, Arnold Electric Co., Racine, Wisconsin, c. 1923. 17-1/2", white, sleeve bearing. Rarity 1, $50-75.

Model 16, Arnold Electric Co., Racine, Wisconsin, c. 1925. 18", beige, sleeve bearing. Rarity 3, $100-150.

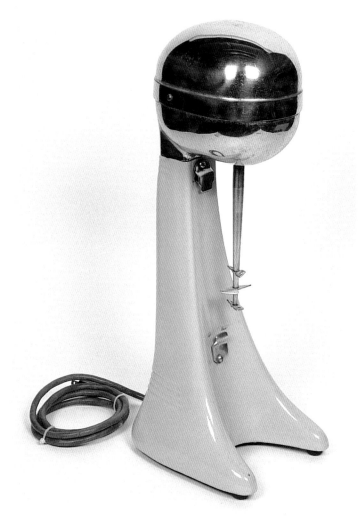

Mixer No. 53, Benedict Mfg. Co., East Syracuse, New York, c. 1945. 18-1/2", green/black, ball bearing. Rarity 2, $100-175.

Unknown, Benedict Mfg. Co., East Syracuse, New York, c. 1950. 19", green, ball bearing. Rarity 4, $200-300.

Mixer No. 58, Benedict Mfg. Co., East Syracuse, New York, c. 1950. 17", green, ball bearing. Rarity 2, $75-125.

CanAm, Canadian Armature Works, Montreal, Canada, c. 1945. 18", beige, ball bearing. Rarity 3, $125-150.

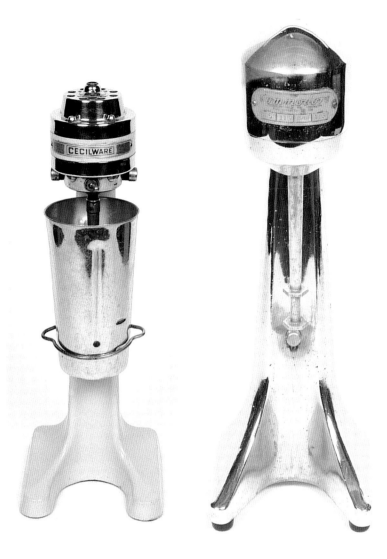

Cecilware, Cecil Mfg. Co., New York, c. 1930. 18", green, sleeve bearing. Rarity 3, $100-150.

Commodore, Commodore Mfg. Co., Toronto, Canada, c. 1945. 17", chrome, ball bearing. Rarity 4, $125-150.

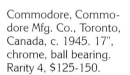

Model B 12, Cecil Mfg. Co., New York, c. 1933. 18-1/2", green, ball bearing. Rarity 2, $80-100.

STAR-Rite Electric Mixer, Fitzgerald Mfg. Co., Torrington, Connecticut, c. 1925. 10"-14-1/2", chrome, sleeve bearing. Rarity 2, $65-85.

Thermomixer, Fulton-Bell
Co., New York, c. 1915.
13"-17-1/2", chrome,
sleeve bearing. Rarity 5,
$300-400.

Hamilton Beach
Cyclone, earliest
model, Racine,
Wisconsin, c. 1912,
12-1/2" x 17-1/2",
sleeve bearing,
nickel plated.
Rarity 2, $150-250.

Gilchrist & Hamilton Beach Model 22, Gilchrist Co., Newark, New Jersey, c. 1925. 17", white, sleeve bearing. Rarity 1, $45-65 each.

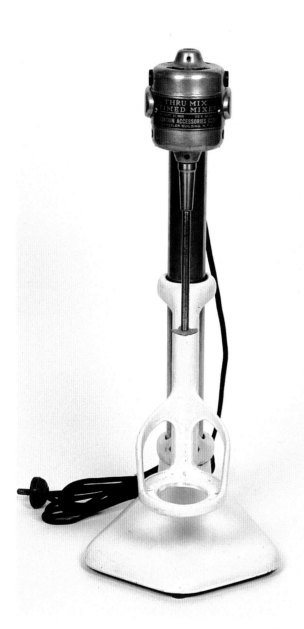

Thru Mix Timed Mixer, Fountain Accessories Corp., New York, c. 1926. 20-1/2", white, sleeve bearing. Rarity 5, $200-250.

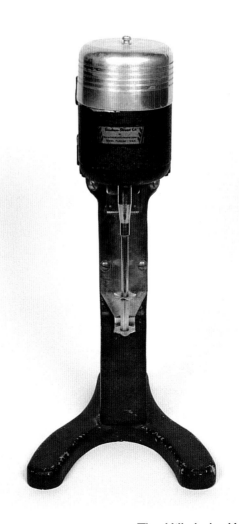

Goodman-Stewart, Goodman-Stewart Co., Miami, Florida, c. 1945, 19", black, ball bearing. Rarity 4, $75-100.

Hamilton Beach Cyclone, early model with marble base, Racine, Wisconsin, c. 1912, 12-1/2" x 17-1/2", sleeve bearing, nickel plated. Rarity 3, $150-250.

Hamilton Beach Light Up, Racine, Wisconsin, c. 1917, 18", sleeve bearing, nickel plated. Rarity 3, $200-300.

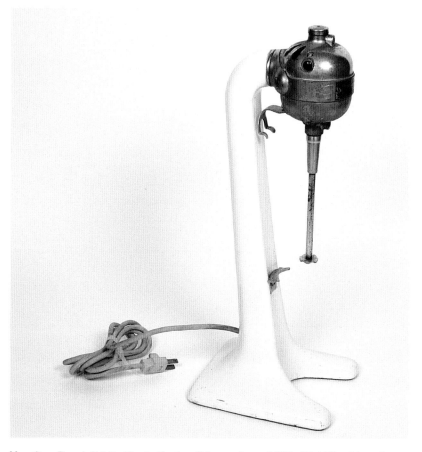

Hamilton Beach Cyclone with mixer raised, Racine, Wisconsin, c. 1912, 12-1/2" x 17-1/2", sleeve bearing, nickel plated. Rarity 3, $150-250.

Hamilton Beach White Flash, Racine, Wisconsin, c. 1920, 17-1/2", white, sleeve bearing. Rarity 2, $90-100.

Hamilton Beach Model 8, shows milkshake cup, Racine, Wisconsin, c. 1925, 17-1/2", white, sleeve bearing. Rarity 3, $90-100.

Hamilton Beach Drinkmaster, beige, Racine, Wisconsin, c. 1929, 18-1/2", ball bearing. Rarity 1, $100-150.

Hamilton Beach Model 17 (Arnold), Racine, Wisconsin, c. 1933, 17-1/2", light green, ball bearing. Rarity 3, $100-150.

Hamilton Beach Model 10, Racine, Wisconsin, c. 1927, 17-1/2", white/green, sleeve bearing. Rarity 3, $75 in white, $100 in colors.

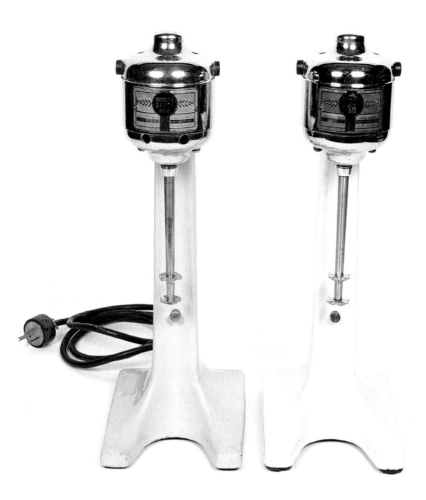

Hamilton Beach Model 27, Racine, Wisconsin, c. 1937, 17-1/2", green, sleeve bearing. Rarity 3, $125-175.

Hamilton Beach Model 18, Racine, Wisconsin, c. 1935, 17-1/2", light green/beige, ball bearing. Rarity 3, $100-150 each.

Hamilton Beach Model 25, Racine, Wisconsin, c. 1937, 18", beige/green/black/red, sleeve bearing. Rarity 1, $100 beige-green, $150 black, $200 red.

Hamilton Beach Model 30, Racine, Wisconsin, c. 1943, 18-1/2", green/beige/black, ball bearing. Rarity 1, $100 green/beige, $150-200 black.

Stafford, J.H. Stafford Industries, Ltd, Toronto, Canada, c. 1945, 17-1/2", polished aluminum, ball bearing. Rarity 4, $150-200.

Hamilton Beach Model 33, Racine, Wisconsin, c. 1943, 17-3/4", green/beige/black, ball bearing. Rarity 1, $100-150 green/beige, $150-200 black.

Model 40, John Oster Mfg. Co., Racine, Wisconsin, c. 1945, 19", green, ball bearing. Rarity 2, $100 no cup, $150 with cup.

Hamilton Beach Model 51, Racine, Wisconsin, c. 1955, 14", white, ball bearing. Rarity 1, $30-40.

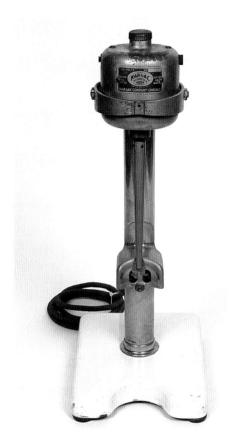

The "Liquid" Mixer,
Liquid Carbonic Co.,
Chicago, Illinois,
c. 1925, 18", white,
sleeve bearing.
Rarity 5, $75-85.

Karlac Hotancold Mixer, Karlac Co. Chicago,
Illinois, c. 1930, 18", white, ball bearing.
Rarity 3, $100-125.

Universal, Landers, Frary &
Clark, New Britain, Con-
necticut, c. 1949, 19", white,
sleeve bearing. Rarity 5,
$350-450.

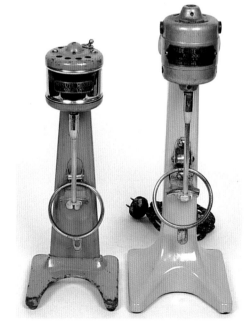

Minute Mixer, Made-Rite Mfg. Co., Sandusky,
Ohio, c. 1935, 14", green, sleeve bearing.
Rarity 3, $75-100; Made-Rite Mixer No. 200,
Made-Rite Mfg. Co., Sandusky, Ohio,
c. 1935, 15-3/4", green, sleeve bearing.
Rarity 3, $125-175.

Champion Mixer Model K1, Premier
Industries Corp., New York, c. 1940,
20", green, ball bearing. Rarity 3,
$100-150.

DeLuxe Drink Mixer, Myers DeLuxe Products
Corp., Galesburg, Illinois, c. 1940, 16-1/2",
green, ball bearing. Rarity 2, $100-150.

Bullet Mixer, Myers DeLuxe Products Corp., Galesburg, Illinois,
c. 1945, 19", green, ball bearing. Rarity 3, $75-100 each.

Champion Mixer Model K4, Premier Industries Corp., New York, c. 1945, 16", green,
ball bearing. Rarity 3, $75-100.

Thur-O- Mixer No. 2, Rex Supply Co., Muskegon, Michigan, c. 1940, 16-1/2", green, ball bearing. Rarity 4, $100-150.

Mix 'n Whip, Racine Electric Products, Racine Wisconsin, c. 1945, 19-1/2", green, ball bearing. Rarity 3, $125-175.

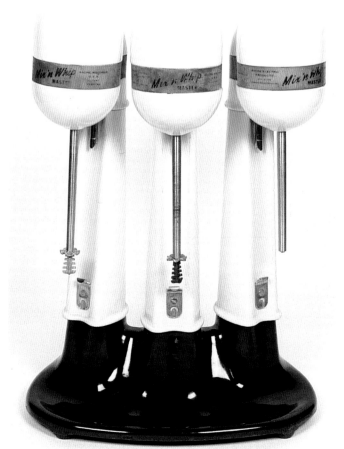

Mix 'n Whip Triple Head, Racine Electric Products, Racine, Wisconsin, c. 1945, 20", white with black base, ball bearing. Rarity 5, $400-600.

Standard Mixer, Standard Products Corp., Whitman, Massachusetts, c. 1945, 18", beige, ball bearing. Rarity 3, $75-125.

Star Mixer Model 181,
Star Mfg. Co., St. Louis,
Missouri, c. 1940,
19-3/4", beige, ball
bearing.
Rarity 3, $150-200.

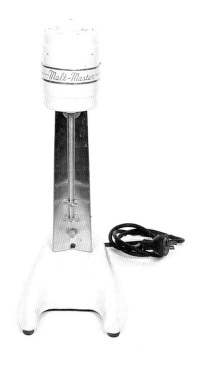

Malt-Master, Van Burt
Electric Co.,
unknown location,
c. 1940, 16-1/2",
pale yellow, ball
bearing.
Rarity 3, $100-125.

Model 100, Stevens Electric Co., Racine,
Wisconsin, c. 1934, 12-1/2", green and
black, ball bearing. Rarity 3, $125-175.

Dumore, Wisconsin Electric Co. Racine,
Wisconsin, c. 1925, 14" – 19-1/2", white,
sleeve bearing. Rarity 5, $600-900.

Horlick's push-down, Wisconsin Electric Co., Racine, Wisconsin,
c. 1925, 13-1/2" – 20", white, sleeve bearing. Rarity 5, $600-900.

Horlick's lift-up, Wisconsin Electric Co., Racine, Wisconsin, c. 1925, 14", black, sleeve bearing. Rarity 3, $125-200.

Chapter 14
Fans for Ladies

Back in the days before air conditioning—yes, there was such a time—ice cream parlors often gave fans to the ladies so they could cool themselves off during the sweltering heat of summer. Most of the fans carried some advertising on the reverse side, usually for an ice cream brand or an ice cream luncheonette.

Shady Lawn Creamery, c. 1920s. $15-20.

c. 1925-1935. $25-50.

DeCoursey Ice Cream, c. 1920s. $15-20.

c. 1925-1935.
$25-50.

c. 1925-1935. $25-50.

c. 1925-1935. $25-50.

c. 1925-1935.
$25-50.

c. 1925-1935.
$25-50.

c. 1925-1935. $25-50.

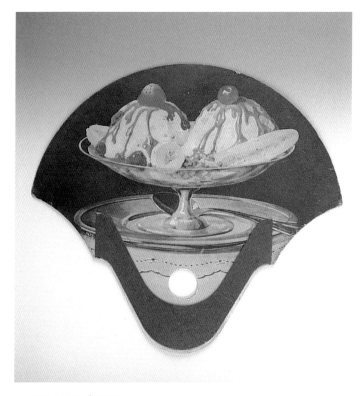

c. 1925-1935. $25-50.

c. 1925-1935. $25-50.

c. 1925-1935. $25-50.

c. 1925-1935. $25-50.

c. 1925-1935. $25-50.

c. 1925-1935. $25-50.

c. 1925-1935. $25-50.

c. 1925-1935. $25-50.

c. 1925-1935. $25-50.

c. 1925-1935. $25-50.

Chapter 15
Ice Cream Valentines

Valentines really require no explanation. Suffice to say that valentines with an ice cream theme or illustration of some type are out there waiting to be found. It's just one of those things you discover as you begin to collect and focus on a theme. While they are not a major collectible category on their own, they are often referred to as "go withs." They go with the theme and are fun. Be mine, oh valentine.

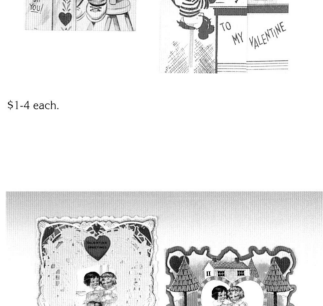

$1-4 each.

$1-4 each.

$1-4 each.

Two old fashioned, c. 1940s. $8-10 each.

$1-4 each.

Comic valentine, $4.

Small valentines, $5 each.

Small valentines $1-5 each.

Valentine child, $15.

Valentine
cutout, $15.

Chapter 16
Hand Cranked Ice Cream Freezers

It is only in the last few years that the birth and growth of the hand cranked ice cream freezer has been fully and officially documented. Nancy Johnson, a Navy wife in Philadelphia, did secure a patent in 1843. Why a housewife, no one knows. It was surely a strange thing for a woman to do in those days. But it did wonders for our ability to make ice cream, primarily reducing the time it took to make a batch of ice cream from hours to minutes.

Prior to the invention of the hand cranked freezer, ice cream had been made everywhere in the world by what was referred to as "the still pot method." This meant that the milk, cream, and sugar were put into a container, usually a pewter pot, and the pot was set on or surrounded by a bed of ice and salt. It was then allowed to sit there until the contents froze. This also meant that the contents needed to be stirred about every half an hour to create what eventually became the scraper action of the blade in Nancy Johnson's machine. It was not unusual for this procedure to take about four hours. This use of ice and salt was called the endothermic theory of freezing. It referred to the fact that the salt on the ice lowered the freezing point to about 22 degrees, well below 32 degrees, the point at which water freezes. Making ice cream was a tedious task from the standpoint that it was quite time consuming. And in those days, batches were made in small quantities, usually about two quarts at a time.

Once most inventions are on the market, others begin to make improvements and create innovations—such was the case with this one. In Johnson's freezer, the canister was stationery. Hand cranking it caused the dasher inside to rotate and scrape the frozen product from the side. Within the next forty years, however, double and triple action freezers were on the market wherein the dasher and canisters both rotated, making the freezing quicker and the product better. By that time, the freezing action had been cut to a matter of minutes.

Around 1868, horizontal freezers had also arrived on the market. In these, the barrel was mounted horizontally. The freezers themselves had a distinctive box or chest-like appearance. As collectibles, they are the most difficult to find.

The other treasure among hand cranked ice cream freezers is what is known as the Salesman's Sample. This is a miniature model that salesmen used as an aid to sell their wares. Originals are also difficult to find and, as with many other collectibles today, reproductions have hit the market.

From a historical point of view you might be interested to know that ice and salt were used in the manufacture of commercial ice cream clear into 1905, when ammonia brine replaced the salt and ice.

Two quart Auto Vacuum. $75-90.

Acme Instant Freezer, 1891. $500-750.

Skerrett Freezer, English. $1,000-1,200.

New Standard Triple Action, Standard Corp., Mount Joy, Pennsylvania. $70-95.

Instantaneous Ice Cream Freezer. $525-600.

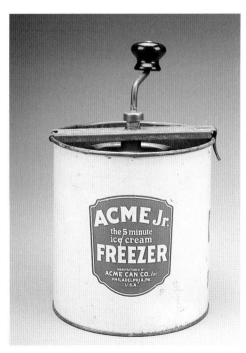

Acme Jr. Ice Cream Freezer, Philadelphia, Pennsylvania. $40-50.

Instant Whip, 1891, Instant Freeze Co., Milwaukee, Wisconsin. $135.

Regal two quart, Mount Joy, Pennsylvania. $55-70.

Instant Freezer Co., 1891, Fitchburg, Massachusetts. $450-525.

Jack Frost horizontal freezer. $500-600.

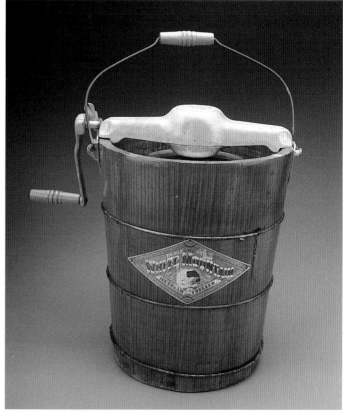

White Mountain Ice Cream Freezer. $95-110.

Reliance Ice Cream Freezer. $125-140.

Peerless Iceland Ice Cream salesman's model. $175-200.

Horizontal Polar Star Instantaneous Ice Cream Freezer. $500-700.

Polar Star Worm Gear horizontal, 1893. $300-500.

Eismaschin
Freezer, Germany.
$75-100.

Chapter 17
Ice Cream Blotters

About fifteen years ago, I was visiting a friend who asked me if I'd recently found any new ice cream collectibles. My response was "Yes, I just bought a half dozen blotters that have ice cream themes on them." With that, his teenage daughter said, "Excuse me, Mr. Marks, but what is a blotter?" It was one of my first realizations that I was no longer a youngster and that there were generations of people out there who grew up with only the ballpoint pen. If you require an explanation of a blotter, skip this section and move on.

Blotters, as explained in the Burdick-Garrison catalog of 1917, were quite often used either as a piece of co-operative dealer work (where the ice cream manufacturer printed the name of his brand and the dealer's advertisement at the bottom) or as a piece of direct advertising mailed directly to the consumer. Actually, I wasn't aware of the fact that they used direct mail advertising back in those ancient times. I thought that was a modern day curse.

Many ice cream manufacturers used a different blotter each month and printed a small monthly calendar along with copy featuring their specials for the month. The blotters were generally 3-1/4" by 6-1/4" inches in size.

Horton's Ice Cream, Furbush's Ice Cream, blank; c. 1930. $15 each.

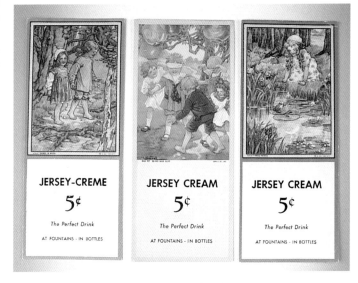

Jersey Cream, set of three; c. 1925. $50 for set.

Velvet Brand Ice Cream, Sheffer's Ice Cream; c. 1925-1930. $15 each.

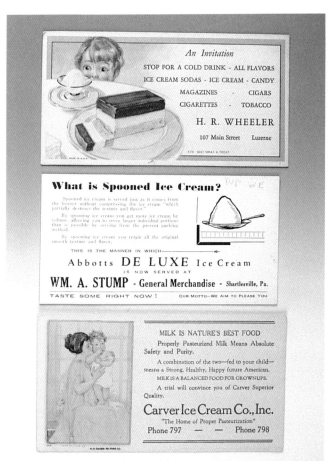

H.R. Wheeler, Spooned Ice Cream, Carver Ice Cream; c. 1930. $15 each.

Chapter 18
Trade Cards

Before the business card became the prevalent means of promoting yourself or your business, the trade card was the dominant item used, starting about 1875. Varying in size from something similar to today's business card up to postcard size, the trade card carried not only business information but also nice illustrations and floral designs to catch your attention. They are not too difficult to find and there are a few trade card associations out there for collectors to join.

Confectionery and ice cream. $12-15 each.

Ice cream parlor/salon. $15 each.

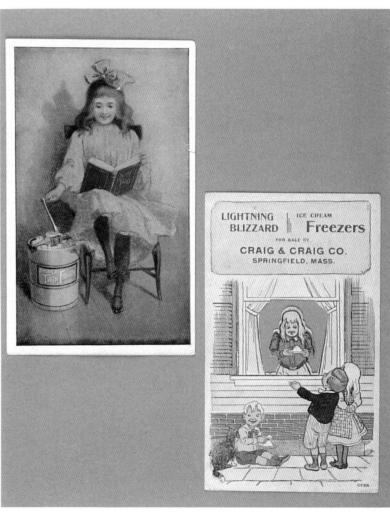

Ice cream freezers. $15 each.

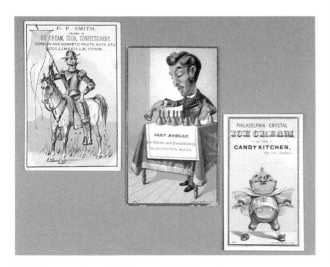

Ice Cream and confectionary. $10-12 each.

American Machine, ice cream freezer. $18 each.

Ice cream. $20-25 each.

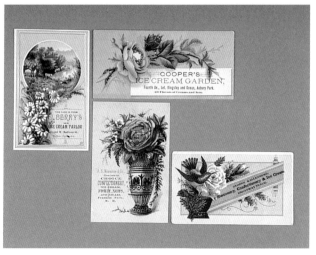

Ice Cream parlors. $12-15 each.

Chapter 19
Ice Cream Postcards

This is a category of ice cream collectibles that could keep you searching forever.

The best place to find them is at postcard shows, which are generally held about twice a year in various locations in conjunction with local postcard clubs. It would not be an exaggeration to say that you could build a collection of 1,500 to 2,000 different ice cream picture postcards if you were to become an avid collector.

What makes it interesting is that there are so many categories you can focus on. For example, there are Kewpie postcards, soda fountain interiors, ice cream manufacturing plants, beach scenes, lots of humorous things, children, the Olde Times, ice cream and the Armed Forces, back on the farm days, romance, family and kids, ice cream socials, and ice cream in foreign lands.

The possibilities are unlimited. If you attend the same postcard shows on a frequent basis you become familiar with the dealers and they start to search for you, bringing their finds to your local show. My collection of foreign ice cream postcards grew in just this fashion.

Kewpie ice cream postcards, Rose O'Neill. $20-30 each.

c. 1910-1920. $25 each.

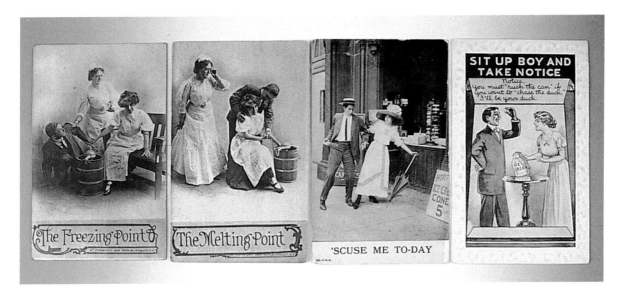

c. 1910-1915. $25 each.

c. 1915. $25 each.

Ice cream plant interior,
c. 1900. $30-35. Horse
drawn delivery wagon,
c. 1900. $30-35.

Foreign ice cream cards, Scottish and English. $10 each.

Foreign ice cream cards, German and French. $10 each.

Above and below:
Childish ice cream humor. $10 each.

A reflection on childhood. $15-20 each.

Comic postcards. $5 each.

Ice Cream manufacturing plants.
$10-15 each.

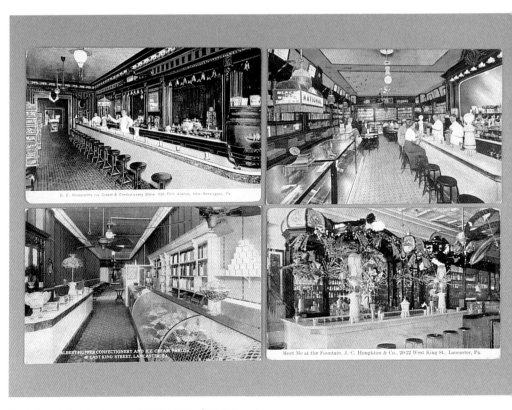

Soda fountain interiors, c. 1910-1925. $15-20 each.

Chapter 20
Business Envelopes

The attraction of business envelopes as an ice cream collectible centers primarily on the cachet found on the envelope. These can vary from business logos to something commemorative. Often they are quite colorful and interesting. Business envelopes are not overly difficult to locate and are a relatively inexpensive sector of the collecting arena.

Ice Screamers 15th Annual Convention; Saint Louis World's Fair Stamp, First Day Issue, Celebration of the Century by the Postal Service. $5 each.

Thomas Mills & Brother Freezers; Automatic Cone Co.; Turnbull's Products; Colonial Ice Cream. $10-15 each.

Purity Ice Cream; Consumers Ice Cream; Gem Freezers; Kendell & Whitney Freezers. $10-15 each.

Timitch Cones; Colonial Ice Cream; Sysco Cones; Thomas Mills & Brother, Inc. $10-15 each.

Chapter 21
Trade Publications

Unlike some of the others, this is a category of ice cream collectibles with a limited attraction—appealing primarily to those who have been involved in the business, as I have for so many years. However, the old publications do have the ability to generate some nostalgia and since they are not too expensive nor too difficult to find, they are well worth the search.

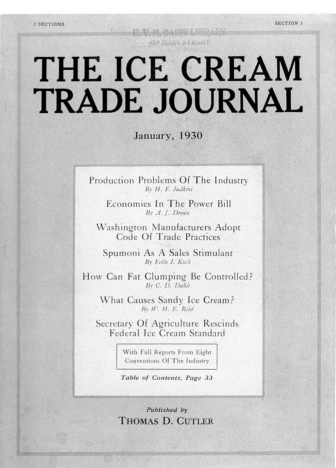

The Ice Cream Trade Journal, January 1930. $15-20.

Ice Cream Field, August 1958. $10.

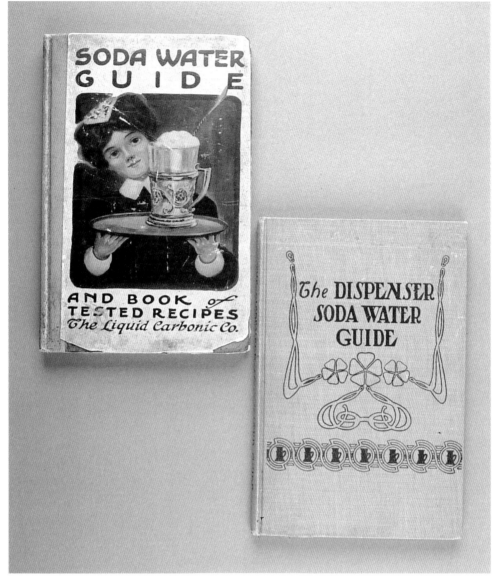

Soda Water Guide and Book of Tested Recipes, Liquid Carbonic
Co., 2nd Edition 1910. $170-200. *The Dispenser Soda Water Guide*,
D.O. Haynes, 1909. $200-220.

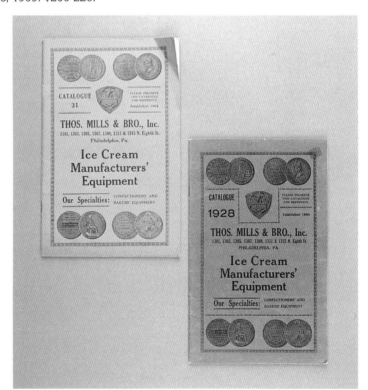

Thomas Mills & Brother, Inc.,
Catalog 31. $100-110.
Thomas Mills & Brother, Inc.,
Catalog 28. $125-135.

Soda Fountain Magazine, March 1931. $25-35.

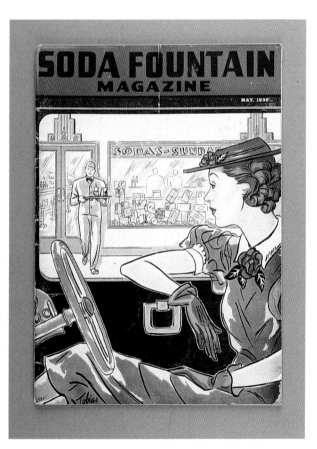

Soda Fountain Magazine, May 1936. $25-30.

Soda Fountain Magazine, November 1929. $25-30.

Chapter 22
Paper Ice Cream Plates

These collectibles were commonly used at ice cream parlors and fountains starting around 1910, before glassware became the common serving dish. About 5-1/2" inches in diameter and fluted to enhance their dish-like quality, they invariably carried the logo or slogan of the ice cream manufacturer. Paper ice cream plates were used quite extensively throughout the 1920s, then became something that just ran out of time.

Swan Ice Cream; Yerdon's Ice Cream – "It's Different"; Kalashian Brother's Velvet Ice Cream. All 5" dia., c. 1920-1938. $15-25 each.

Freeman's Quality Ice Cream; Abbott's Ice Cream; Smith's Ice Cream. All 5" dia., c. 1920-1938. $15-25 each.

Dove Brand Ice Cream – "Delightfully Velvety"; Hood's Ice Cream – "The Flavor's There"; Plymouth Rock Ice Cream – "It's Good For the Children." All 5" dia., c. 1920-1938. $15-25 each.

Turnbull's Green Mountain; Hendler's Ice Cream – "The Velvet Kind"; Ziegenfelder's Ice Cream. All 5" dia., c. 1920-1938. $15-25 each.

Chapter 23
Ice Cream Cartons

In the early days, when ice cream was sold primarily at the drugstore fountain or at the confectionery store, it was essentially consumed at the time of sale. It was difficult to take home because *getting* home took much longer than it does today. In addition, if you did get the ice cream home before it melted, keeping it for any length of time was difficult because all the average home had was an ice box, not a freezer.

Well, all that changed as time went by, but the change took place in slow steps. Ice cream was first hand packed in small containers, many of which had string handles so that they could be held almost like a pail. The sizes were small; 4 ounce, 8 ounce, and 16 ounce were the ones most commonly used.

As the retail business developed and gained strength, containers used for ice cream changed in size, shape, and design. Cylindrical pints and quarts became standard, with a change to rectangular evolving next.

By the end of World War II, as supermarkets began to appear and as the average household achieved ownership of a freezer, the half gallon package began to replace the pints and quarts of those early days.

Sizes changed once again when premium ice creams hit the marketplace and manufacturers were able to satisfy consumer demand for something special by using smaller packages.

Sanida Pure Vanilla Ice Cream, quart, horizontal. $18-20.

Producer's Ice Cream, quart. $10-12; Dolly Madison, pint. $10-12; Lockwood's Ice Cream, pint, metal rim. $12-14.

Square Pak, half gallon. $15-18.

Eskimo Pie, carton. $22-25.

Harding's Ice Cream pail, string handle, quart. $15-17; Generic ice cream pail, quart. $10-12.

Pet Ice Cream, 8 ounce cup. $4-6; McMinn's Ice Cream, 8 ounce cup. $6-8.

Levengood's Ice Cream, pint. $5-7; Cream Top Ice Cream, quart. $8-10; Gollam's Ice Cream, pint. $5-7.

Assorted brands, 4 ounces. $6 each.

Generic brand, pint. $4-6; North Pole, quart. $6-8; Van's Dairy, pint. $5-7.

Generic, pint pail. $15-17; Hupper's Ice Cream, quart pail. $12-14; Coon's Ice Cream, half pint container. $17-19.

Bing Crosby, pint. $20-25.

Generic, colonial décor, pint. $15-$18; Ice cream box. $12-14.

Chapter 24
Ice Cream Advertising

This category of collectibles is almost limitless in variety. It includes such an extraordinary range of choices that paper and advertising shows are sure to continually attract you as you establish and build your collection.

Early advertising was essentially conducted by using the local newspapers. When commercial ice cream manufacturers came on the scene, things such as posters, point of sale material, banners, brochures, fancy menus, and special occasion and holiday pieces were all used to woo the housewife. Colorful, unusual, innovative, and attractive they soon became part of our ice cream culture.

Ice Cream Social notice, c. 1884, 12" x 18". $35-45; Ice Cream - An Invitation, c. 1881, 6" x 10". $35-40.

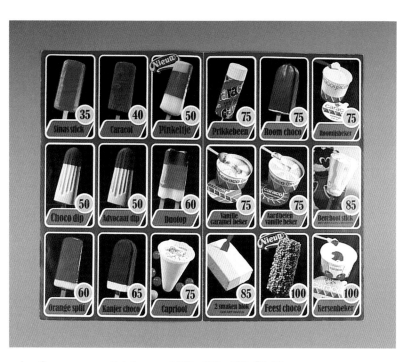

Ice Cream menu, Belgium, c. 1990, 12" x 18". $5-10.

Soda Fountain menu, c. 1950s, 8" x 10". $10-13.

Rich Valley Ice Cream Co. ad sheet, "June Dairy Month Special," c. 1940s, 15" x 12". $15-20.

Superior Brand Ice Cream die cut, c. 1960s, 10" x 18". $15-20.

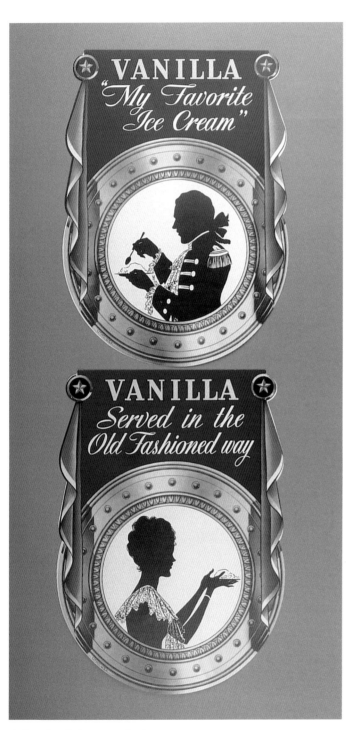

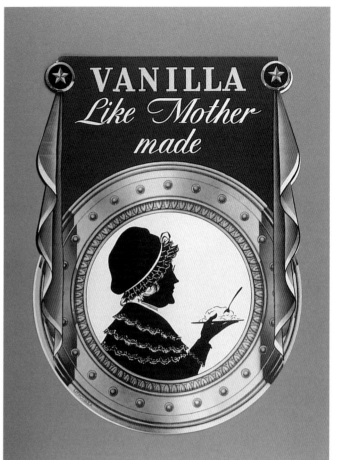

Colonial style hanging ice cream sign,
c. 1940s, 12" x 18". $45-55.

Colonial style hanging duplex ice cream signs,
c. 1940s. $45-55 each.

Whistler's Mother, Mother's Day ice cream sign, set of three, c.
1940s. $85-100 each.

Borden's Ice Cream "Valentine Ice Cream Heart" poster, c. 1935-1945. $25-30.

Ice Cream Kewpie pieces, c. 1935-1945. $15-25 each.

Ice Cream Jack o' Lantern poster, c. 1945-1950, 12" x 18". $15-20.

Borden's Egg Center Ice Cream poster, c. 1940s, 8" x 15". $10-15.

Borden's Egg Nog Ice Cream poster,
c. 1930s, 12"x 24". $10-15.

Frosted Malted, c. 1950, 12" x 18". $12-15.

Eskimo Pie 10¢, c. 1940s, 8" x 14". $15-20; Eskimo Pie
5¢ decal, c. 1930s, 6" dia. $20-25.

Giant Sandwich, c. 1920s, 18" x 24". $15-20.

Chocolate Sundae back bar signs, c. 1940s. $15-20 each.

Fruit Salad Sundae back bar sign, c. 1940s. $5-8.

Burgundy Cherry and Pineapple Sundae back bar signs, c. 1940, 14" oval shape. $8 -12 each.

Butterscotch, Marshmallow and Hot Fudge Sundae set, c. 1950. $15-20 each.

Tarzan Ice Cream Cups, 5¢ wall sign,
c. 1930s, 12"x 24". $35-45.

Tarzan Ice Cream Cup 5¢ wall sign, c. 1930s, 12" x 24". $15-20;
Tarzan Custard Ice Cream Cups, c. 1930s. $15-20.

MelOrol 5¢ Ice Cream Cone poster,
Horns Supreme Ice Cream, c. 1930,
28" x 12". $50-65.

Picaninny Freeze 5¢, c. 1930s, 11" x 14". $75-100.

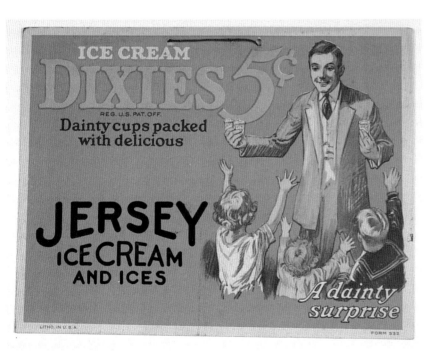

Enjoy Haines CeBrook Ice Cream metal sign, c. 1935, 8" x 14". $10-15.

Ice Cream Dixies, Jersey Ice Cream cardboard sign, c. early 1940s, 10" x 12". $35-45.

Ice Cream Snowballs magazine ad, c. 1938. $5-8.

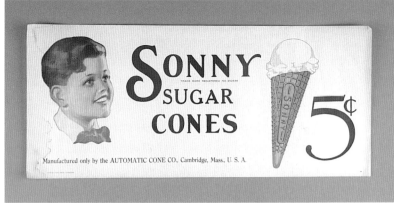

Sonny Sugar Cones, 5¢, c. 1930, 8" x 14". $10-12.

Eskimo Pie magazine ads, c. 1956. $10-12 each.

Dairylea Ice Cream, "Packed in Sanitary Container at the Plant" cardboard poster, c. 1930, 18" x 22". $20-25.

Eskimo Pie countertop sales thermos, "Kept Cold with Magic Ice," c. 1935, 18" tall. $1,200-1,500.

Eskimo Pie countertop sales thermos, "Bracing as a Frosty Morning," c. 1935, 18" tall. $1,200-1,500.

Chapter 25
Ice Cream Trays

In the early days of the ice cream luncheonette, during the period from about 1915-1940, waitress service was a standard part of the service provided by the soda fountain operators. During those years, mothers with their children, ladies with their friends and beaus, and wives with their husbands and family were the major part of the afternoon and early evening trade.

Service was a standard feature, almost as significant as the soda fountain treats themselves. And one of the things that highlighted that service was the attractive trays used by the waitresses to carry the treats that had been ordered.

Early trays showed mothers and children in beautiful color—family scenes, family parties, and ice cream festivities. Men were seldom, if ever, shown. As is true of so much in the business climate, family portrayal eventually dissolved into stark commercialism; company names and logos then began to dominate.

As collectibles, trays are treasured pieces today. While the later ones with company names and logos are not as desirable as those they replaced, they are still sought after by collectors.

Hermes All Cream Ice Cream, oval. $145-165.

Worden's Delicious Ice Cream, 14" diameter. $145-165.

Castles Heathized Ice Cream, 11" x 17". $75-95.

Marrow's Ice Cream. $75-110.

Arctic Ice Cream, oblong. $225-275.

Hall Co's. Quality Ice Cream, 10" x 13". $750-900.

Russ Brothers Velvet Ice Cream, 10" x 13". $750-850.

Hendler's Ice Cream, Kewpie, 11"x 17". $275-325.

Sheffer's Ice Cream, "The taste Tells," 14" dia. $150-190.

Purity Maid Ice Cream, 13" square. $200-275.

Binghamton Ice Cream Co., O. K.
Ice Cream, 5" oval tip tray.
$450-550.

Robin Brand Carbonated
Ice Cream, 14" diameter.
$875-1,000.

Chapter 26
Ice Cream Silverware

This is the silverware of a time gone by. Prior to the Great Depression of the 1930s, when those who were considered wealthy sat down to enjoy their ice creams—whether at a social affair with friends or a catered affair at their club or at one of the better class hotels such as the Waldorf Astoria—the silver they used was sterling silver.

The sterling silver standard was introduced by Tiffany in 1852 and adopted by the U.S. government in 1865 as a standard for United States silver.

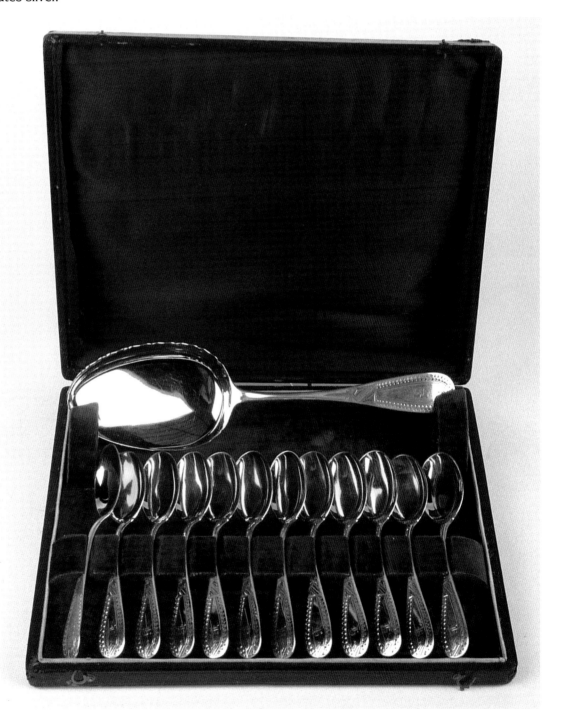

Coin silver ice cream serving set with gold wash, manufactured by Farrington & Hunnewell of Boston; manufacturers mark "F & H" appears on the pieces. $400-500.

Bibliography

Books
Bunn, Eleanore. *Metal Molds*. Paducah, KY: Collectors Books, 1981.

David, Elizabeth. *Harvest of the Cold Months*. London, England: Penguin Groups, 1994.

David, Elizabeth. *Italian Food*. London, England: Barrie & Jenkins, Ltd., 1954.

Dickson, Paul. *The Great American Ice Cream Book*. New York: Anthenum Publishing, 1972.

Funderburg, Ann Cooper. *Chocolate, Strawberry & Vanilla*. Bowling Green, Ohio: Bowling Green State University Popular Press, 1995.

Heacock, William, and William Gamble. *Encyclopedia of Victorian Colored Pattern Glass*, Book #9. Marietta, Ohio: Antique Publications, 1987.

Hiss, Emil A. *Standard Manual of Soda and Other Beverages*. Chicago, IL: G.P. Englehard & Co., 1897.

Kyle, Husfloen. *Collector's Guide To American Pressed Glass, 1825-1915*. Radnor, PA: Wallace-Homestead Book Co., 1992.

Liddell, Caroline, & Robin Weir. *Ices, The Definitive Guide*. London, England: Hodder & Slaughton, 1993.

Liddell, Caroline, & Robin Weir. *Frozen Desserts*. London, England: Hodder & Slaughton, 1996.

Selitzer, Ralph. *The Dairy Industry in America*. New York Magazines for Industry, 1976.

Smith, Wayne. *Ice Cream Dippers*. Walkersville, MD: Wayne Smith, 1986.

Wilson, Steve. *Ice Cream Freezers*. Fayetteville, AR: Steve Wilson, 1996.

Periodicals
American Soda Book. American Soda Fountain Co., Boston, MA, n.d.

The Dispenser's Formulary or Soda Water Guide, 3rd Edition, revised. D.O. Haynes, New York, 1915.

Soda Fountain Trade Magazine. New York, Soda Fountain Publications Inc., June 1925.

Ice Cream Trade Journal. Trade Paper Division of Rueben Donnelley Corp., Philadelphia, PA, July 1939.

Collins, Tom. "Straw Holders." *The Ice Screamer*. Issues #63 and #64, August & November 1994.

Catalogs
V. Clad & Sons. Philadelphia, PA, 1911.

Thomas Mills & Brother. Philadelphia, PA, 1912.

Burdick & Garrison. New York, 1918.